THE DEFINITIVE GUIDE TO

GREEK MYTHOLOGY

MOSELEY ROAD INC.
International Rights and Packaging
32 N. Dutcher St.,
Irvington, NY 10533
www.moseleyroad.com
President Sean Moore
International Rights, Karen Prince: kprince@moseleyroad.com

Series editors: Fiona Baile and Duncan Youel
Art direction: Duncan Youel at oiloften.co.uk
Design: Philippa Baile at oiloften.co.uk

ISBN 978-1-62669-222-0

Printed in China

10 9 8 7 6 5 4 3 2 1   21 22 23 24 25

THE DEFINITIVE GUIDE TO

GREEK
MYTHOLOGY

THE GODS, HEROES, MONSTERS
AND LEGENDS OF ANCIENT GREECE

Rowan Bartlett | Fiona Baile

Moseley Road Inc.

CONTENTS

From its founding of the European philosophic tradition to its innovations in the dramatic arts, architecture and sculpture, Ancient Greece was the rosy-fingered dawn of western civilization.

ANCIENT GREECE

GULF OF VENICE

ITALY

ALBANIA

MACEDON or COMINOLTART

IONIAN SEA

ISLE OF CORFU

GREECE

THESSALY

JANNA

EGI

ISLE OF EGRIPO

SALONICA

Gulf of Katchiera

LEFCATHIA

Isle of Sta Maura

CEFALONIA
Gr. Kephalonia

LIVADIA

GULF OF LEPANTO or Corytho

ZANT
Ital. Zante

MOREA

NEGROPONTE

ATHENS

GULF OF NAPOLI or ARGOS

SEA OF SAPIENZA

GULF OF CORON

GULF OF MIRATONISI or of Coladina

C. Matapan
Tænarum Prom.

CERIGO

MEDITERRANEAN

CRITI

Turc. AK

GREECE,
ARCHIPELAGO
AND
PART OF ANADOLI.
By L. S. DE LA ROCHETTE,
MDCCXC.
LONDON.
Published for Will. FADEN,
Geographer to the KING.
January 1st
1791.

In this Map, or rather Geographical Essay,
Morea and the adjacent parts are delineated according to
the Drawing of the German Engineer Nähmet von Bottmersdorf in the Venetian
Service, a curious Manuscript obligingly communicated by some late Travellers,
to whom also we owe a multitude of New and interesting Details
in the several districts of Greece, Macedonia &c.
as well as in the Archipelago,
and on the Western and Southern coasts of Anadoli.
For the Country round Athens, or Ancient Attica; the Passes of
the Thermopylæ and of the Valley of Tempe, with the
surrounding Parts, and for the Isles of Zant & Negroponte,
Use has been made of the Papers of Mr Stuart.

The Ancient Names are underlined
or Lycione.

8

Longitude East of London

Ancient Greece appeals to all the intellectual values we hold dear in our culture, yet woven into this majestic and luxurious fabric of early enlightenment were protracted periods of blood-soaked, primitive warfare. Out of this great amalgam of events tumbled a cornucopia of gods, myths and monsters, replete with a body of epic legends of heroes and heroines.

ANCIENT GREECE

ABOVE: Paleolithic men hunting reindeer with a spear and bow and arrows.

Some two thousand years later, the old Greek civilization was to beguile the Florentine painters, sculptors, and architects, who rediscovered Classical Antiquity in the fifteenth century, and who brought forth its rebirth in the Italian *Renaissance*. Ancient Greek words, terms and references color our language today, and reveal that they are enduring metaphors for life in our western tradition.

Greece lies in the north-eastern Mediterranean Sea, at the crossroads of Africa, Asia and Europe, and its geography meant its inhabitants were well placed for voyages to all points around the Mediterranean region. An intricate trading network grew up on and around the Greek mainland and its Peloponnese peninsula; the islands of Crete and Cyprus; and the many dozens of smaller islands which became home to the ancient Greeks.

NEOLITHIC PERIOD
C.12,000 TO 3,500 BC

In the mists of pre-history—the Paleolithic, or Old Stone Age, humans were hunter-gatherers who survived by hunting, fishing and gathering plants—a nomadic, wandering existence in which day-to-day survival was paramount. With the discovery of primitive farming around 12,000 BC, (which defines the beginning of the Neolithic era), fixed human settlements slowly began to appear. The earliest evidence of burial sites in the Aegean have been dated to around 7,250 BC, and ancient stone tools, which have been discovered in Macedonia and the Peloponnese peninsula of mainland Greece, support the existence of Paleolithic and Mesolithic (Middle Stone Age) societies. Archaeological evidence also exists of the inhabitation of the Acropolis (literally "high city") of Athens dating back to 4,000 BC. The rocky outcrop originally bore the name Cecropia, after the mythical serpent-man Cecrops, said to be the first king of Athens, whilst its eastern flank was surrounded by the Wooded Hill of the Nymphs.

THE EARLY BRONZE AGE
C.3,500 BC

At first, these settlements were small, isolated, self-governing tribes which developed culturally and politically at different rates. Crafts began to be discernible, notably stone masonry, early metal-working, jewelry-making, and pottery. As people and tribes began to specialize, trade emerged and settlements grew into small cities.

THE MINOAN PERIOD
C.3,200 TO C.1100 BC

The existence of a sophisticated, flourishing society on ancient Crete was discovered by the British archaeologist Sir Arthur Evans, from 1900–1905, when he organised the excavations at Knossos. The labyrinth-like maze of rooms called to mind the myth of King Minos and the Minotaur, and Evans named this very old society "Minoan."

The Minoan Civilization, situated mainly on the island of Crete, was the first such Bronze Age civilization in Europe (though Stonehenge, the Bronze Age solstice monument in Wiltshire, England, has been dated back to an almost similar time.) Its sophisticated urban civilization, built on an extensive network of trade across much of the Mediterranean and the Near East, constructed great palace complexes which incorporated water control and plumbing systems. Minoan palaces were often four storeys high—incredible feats of early engineering. The capital was at Knossos, "Europe's oldest city," on the north coast of Crete, close to the modern city of Heraklion, and other important population centers were Phaistos, Malia, Zakros, and Akrotiri—on the fateful island of Thera (today's Santorini).

The Minoan influence reached as far as Egypt, and Cyprus, in the eastern Mediterranean, from where the Minoans acquired their copper for metalworking. Recent evidence has begun to emerge that 5,000 years ago the region was a little cooler, and wetter. They cultivated fruit orchards and extensive olive groves, whilst also domesticating bees for honey. Their crops ranged from barley and wheat, figs, and grapes. Both wine and honey were a staple part of their trading produce. Their animal husbandry included cattle—bulls were greatly prized, and even revered, but mainly goats, sheep and pigs. Minoan culture held physical sports in high esteem and their wall frescoes and decorated pottery depicted running, wrestling and bull-leaping competitions—a particularly Minoan preoccupation.

At some point between 1600–1400 BC the Minoan culture was sent into terminal decline by a stupendous natural disaster event on Thera, the southern-most island of the Cyclades, just 90 miles from Crete. The catastrophic volcanic eruption is thought to be almost the largest in human history, and almost four times the tremendous size of the well-known Krakatoa explosion of 1883. Preceded by weeks of earthquakes and warning

TOP: Cecrops, an earth born king of Attika and founder of the city of Athens. He had a serpent's tail and the body of a man. He was the first to offer sacrifices to the goddess Athena

MIDDLE: Prehistoric men smelting bronze.

ABOVE: Village showing early bronze age life with farmers, hunters and a man working with bronze.

TOP LEFT: View of the Minoan Palace of Knossos, Crete, Greece.

TOP RIGHT: The ruins of the Temple of Apollo with its Doric columns, Parnassos mountain, Greece. It dates back to the 4th century BC

ABOVE MIDDLE: Sir Arthur John Evans, the British archaeologist, most famous for unearthing the Palace of Knossos, Crete, Greece.

ABOVE: A fresco on a wall at the Palace of Knossos showing a bull with men leaping over it.

signs, vulcanologists have now calculated that the Thera Eruption had four stages across several days, with the final, cataclysmic phase resulting in the collapse of the enormous undersea magma chamber. This last seizmic explosion triggered colossal megatsunamis throughout the Mediterranean, but which hit the north coast of Crete square on. The settlement of Akrotiri, actually on the island of Thera, had already been destroyed, and the great waves deluged all the Minoan cities on the north coast of Crete. The gigantic plumes and final explosion sent out over 14 cubic miles of *tephra*—dense rock, lava bombs, pumice, cinders and ash—into the upper atmosphere, blotting out the sun across the entire region for months. For the Mediterranean region, it was apocalypse. On land, crops for many miles around were submerged under the fallout of dozens of feet of rock and ash, and the resulting *volcanic winter* significantly affected the climate. A widespread famine ensued. Archaeological evidence of the global reach of the Thera explosion has been found in Iceland and documented in China. There are visual records of it on ancient Egyptian pottery. There is much speculation that the build-up to the awesome and deeply frightening stages of the Eruption, the volcanic lightning, the columns of the enormous ash plume stretching up to the heavens, the earthquakes—that all these features down the years became the root source for the central Greek myth of the *Titanomachy*—the Titans' Battle. It's also thought that the megatsunamis were the events behind the creation of the long-standing myth of Atlantis.

MYCENAEAN GREECE C.1750 TO C.1150 BC

The Mycenaean culture was based on the Greek mainland, and is recognized as the first distinctively Greek civilization to have grown up there. The Culture's principal site was at Mycenae, on the Peloponnese peninsula, but evidence of further urban centers were found in Athens; further north in Macedonia; and various outposts in the Aegean Sea, stretching as far as Cyprus in the Eastern Mediterranean; and Italy, far away in the western Mediterranean.

On the slopes of Mount Parnassus in central Greece lay the Mycenaean stronghold at Delphi. This was a "sacred precinct" which the Mycenaean Greeks considered to be the center of the world. It was the seat of the high priestess Pythia—the oracle of Delphi—who was consulted over important decisions throughout the ancient Greek world. Delphi took its name from the Delphyne, the she-serpent who resided there and who was put to death by the god Apollo.

Stories and events in the world were the preserve of the wandering poets, and were told by them to gatherings as they traveled from village to village. As the only means of relating distant events, the Oral Poetic Tradition goes well back into prehistory. The Mycenaeans did develop a form of syllabic script writing, *Linear B*, which they had adapted from the Minoan *Linear A* system (which has never been deciphered), though it's thought that its use was exclusively by scribes for administration purposes. As with the Minoans, athletic competition and religious sports festivals to honor and pay tribute to the gods was an integral part of the Mycenaean world.

Historians now divide the Civilization into three distinct periods: the Early Mycenaean (c.1750–1400 BC); the Palatial Bronze Age (c.1400–c.1250 BC); and the Postpalatial Bronze Age (c.1250–c.1150 BC).

*Some 500 years later, at the outset of the Classical Age, the Mycenaean era would be the historical setting for Homer's epic poems the *Iliad* and the *Odyssey*.

THE LATE BRONZE AGE COLLAPSE
C.1250 TO 1150 BC

Across a fifty to hundred year period, in around 1250–1150 BC, a societal disintegration occurred in the Mediterranean region which archaeologists and historians have called the Late Bronze Age Collapse. It has been characterized by mass migrations and movements of peoples across the Mediterranean world. Various explanations have been offered—frequent earthquake activity which re-routed the natural flow of rivers, silted and drying lakes, crop failure, famine, invasions even, though all these could have been caused by climate shift—and in turn, a possible long-term consequence of the Thera Eruption. Greece and its islands sit on a major junction of the Arabian and Eurasian tectonic plates.

THE GREEK DARK AGES
C.1150 TO C.800 BC

A continuation of the Late Bronze Age Collapse, the so-called Greek Dark Ages chart the rapid decline of the Mycenaean age in Greece. Their palaces were either destroyed, or fell into disuse. The Hittite civilization in Anatolia (present-day Turkey) was similarly affected:—cities from the fabled Troy (present-day Hissarlik on the north-west coast of Turkey) to Gaza in Palestine were abandoned, and even the mighty nation of Egypt fell into disarray. Across the region, great centers of population were dispersed. What's clear is that much of the Mediterranean population didn't survive. In Greece, cultural cohesion

fell apart. After the great societal reach of the Mycenaeans came a 350-year-long decline. The arts disappeared and the administration of society was abandoned. Writing ceased. The conditions for sustaining life had contracted back to pre-Mycenaean levels. There were fewer settlements and societies dwindled, becoming *local*. From around 900 BC, the holy island of Delos, where Dionysus and Leto (the mother of Apollo and Artemis) were venerated, soon became a major cult center. Many Greeks would make the pilgrimage across the Aegean Sea, in the hope of better days ahead.

ARCHAIC GREECE
C.800 TO C.500 BC

The structural beginnings of the Classical Age of Greece were put in place during the hundred year period of the 8th century BC, and necessary fundamental changes in Greek society took place, as it slowly emerged from the Dark Ages. It began with an upsurge in the population, which fostered the revolution that established the *polis*—the famed city-state. This urbanizing process, which united small villages into discrete kingdoms, was in train during

ABOVE: Heinrich Schliemann, a pioneer of archaeology. He believed that Homer's *Iliad* reflected historical events, and was keen to excavate these areas of interest.

TOP: A gold mask of Agamemnon, discovered by Heinrich Schliemann in 1876 in Greece.

much of the 8th century BC. There grew to be over 1000 city-states, with the major centers being Athens, Sparta, Corinth, Thebes, and Eretria.

Alongside this major shift, the Greek alphabet was devised, and the earliest surviving Greek literature was written. Sea trade links were re-established, Athens began development of a navy, and structural reforms in the military were implemented as young men were required to undertake military service. The concept of the citizen-soldier, the *hoplite*, appeared, together with an innovative infantry strategy. The *phalanx formation*, taken up by commanders of the new city-state armies, made soldiers more efficient in defense *and* offense— using 18-feet long *sarissa* spears behind their shield walls as they moved to the attack. The hoplites were primarily citizens, and made up the bulk of ancient Greek armies.

Religious festivals of sport which honored the gods had been part of Greek life since the Minoans, over 2,000 years before, but in 776 BC these were now formalized into a four-year cycle—the Panhellenic Games, and split across four of the new city-states: Olympia, Nemea, Isthmia and Delphi. They were played out to pay tribute to Zeus, king of the gods, as well as to remember their heroes, comrades in arms who had fallen in battle. Oxen were sacrificed at the altar of a huge, 40-foot tall gold and ivory statue of Zeus and great banquets were had. Around 700 BC the poet Hesiod (c.750–c.670 BC) wrote down the *Theogony*, ancient Greece's first documented creation story and succession myth. A poetic synthesis of stories passed down from the Mycenaean era, it tells how the

gods took control of the universe. Hesiod is also credited with establishing many ancient Greek religious customs. Many new temples were built, with early wooden structures now replaced by marble and stone. In the shift to durable materials, proportions were further developed and based around an entrance entablature, typically containing a frieze dedicated to the deity, on columnar supports. It became the archetype. Originating in the western Doric region, the style of column was economic, and popular, becoming widely used, and known since antiquity as the Doric Order.

Working at a similar time to Hesiod, the poet Homer (c.780–c.700 BC) wrote his epic poems the *Iliad* and the *Odyssey*. Set in Mycenaean Greece, 500 years in the past, the *Iliad* describes the final weeks of the Trojan War. The *Odyssey* tells of the subsequent fantastical adventures of the hero Odysseus, king of Ithaca, who has not yet returned from the Trojan War, and his family still wait for him. Its key themes are: *Wandering*; *Testing*; *Omens*; and *Return*.

The Greeks' predilection for the Oral Tradition and the telling of stories found a fixed home in Athens. The city-state had become the dominant cultural, political, and religious center from around 700 BC onwards, and the *Dionysia*, a religious festival honoring the god Dionysus, became a significant event where stories were told and sung—but eventually began to be enacted. The genres and forms of Western theater evolved here: the *heroic*; the *comic*; *tragedy*, and the *absurd* were all crystallized at this time as a means of articulating and asserting the fundamental truths of the human condition. Aeschylus

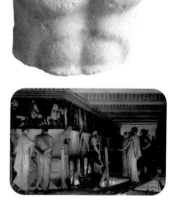

(c.525–455 BC), the Attican playwright and soldier, expanded the numbers of characters and allowed conflict between them. He was a key figure in the development of tragedy plays. Subsequently, Athenian dramatist Sophocles (497–406 BC) discovered the groundbreaking technique of *tragic irony*. Satyr plays with their mythological-heroic stories were also performed in the Dionysia festivals.

Early Greek philosophy began in the 6th century BC with Thales (c.623–c.545 BC), Xenophanes (c.570–c.478 BC), Heraclitus "the Obscure" (c.535–c.475 BC), Pythagoras (570–485 BC), and Parmenides (c.515 BC). This new type of Greek sought intellectual explanations of the world based on cosmology and the natural sciences, rather than the whims of the gods. Heraclitus and Parmenides became well-known for their *metaphysics*—defining the nature of reality, though they were also considered *mystics*—dedicated to the attainment of insight into hidden truths. With the continued rise of philosophy, the fate of the great myths became uncertain. Whilst poets and dramatists were reworking them, Greek philosophers and historians were beginning to unpick them.

These major figures ushered in the Classical Age of ancient Greece, with Athens at its center.

THE CLASSICAL AGE C.500 TO 323 BC

Defined by historian Anthony Snodgrass as Greece's "intellectual revolution," the great flowering of the ancient Greek civilization coincided, somewhat paradoxically, with the opening skirmishes in a bloody and destructive

war against the *Achaemenid* empire—the mighty Persian empire, that would span some fifty years. In 500 BC the Persian empire encompassed much of the ancient world of the Middle East, Arabia, Central Asia, Egypt (where the Persian kings ruled as pharaohs), and Anatolia/Asia Minor, the western coast of which, Ionia, bordering on the Aegean sea, was inhabited by Greeks.

By 492 BC Darius the Great, the Persian king, had set his sights on the conquest of Greece. However, in 490 BC, the invading Persians, commanded by Mardonius, were decisively beaten by the Athenian hoplites at the Battle of Marathon. Darius died before the Persians could make any further incursions, and his son, Xerxes took up the challenge of subjugating Greece. He amassed "the greatest army and navy ever seen" and, in the spring of 480 BC entered Greece from the north. A small allied Greek force, led by the Spartan king Leonidas and 300 of his handpicked warriors, engaged the Persian hordes at the narrow coastal pass of Thermopylae. Leonidas and the 300 entered the annals of eternal legend as they died at a last stand after three days of resistance. The Persians then entered Attica, and made their way to the now evacuated Athens—which they sacked and burned. However, whilst seeking to destroy the Greek navy, the Persian fleet suffered a major defeat at the Battle of Salamis. 12 months later, the allied Greek armies regrouped, went on the offensive and decisively defeated the Persians at the Battle of Plataea. This great success was followed up by the destruction of the remaining Persian fleet, which ended Persian aggression.

TOP LEFT: Marble bust of Aeschylus, circa 30 BC. He is often described as the father of tragedy.

TOP RIGHT: An early form of photography, a daguerreotype, taken of the Acropolis in Athens, Greece. By Joseph-Philibert Girault de Prangey 1842.

ABOVE MIDDLE: Leonidas, king of Sparta circa 489 BC. He led the allied Greek forces at the battle of Thermopylae.

ABOVE RIGHT: Phidias, a Greek sculptor, showing his friends the frieze of the Parthenon. Painted by Lawrence Alma Tadema, 1868.

TOP RIGHT: Bust of the ancient Greek general and historian Thucydides from the Royal Ontario Museum.

MIDDLE: Roman bust of Herodotos; Stone Sculpture; 2nd Century A.D. (copy of a Greek bronze statue made in first half of the fourth century B.C)

ABOVE: Folio from the second edition of Thomas Hobbes' translation Thucydides, The History of the Grecian War, 1676

Much of the historical record of the extended war with Persia comes from Herodotus (c.484–425 BC), who became known as "the father of history." During the Persian sacking of Athens, the Old Temple of Athena, one of several temples sited on the Acropolis, was destroyed. However, in 447 BC Pericles (c.495–429 BC), the Athenian statesman and former general, would coordinate the construction, and reconstruction, of many buildings on the iconic hill, including the Parthenon, the Propylaea, the Erechtheion and the Temple of Athena Nike. Today this version of the Parthenon is the most important surviving building of Classical Greece, and the high point of Doric Order architecture.

Between 460–445 BC, and then again between 431–404 BC, the immense friction generated between the two great city-states of ancient Greece—Athens and Sparta, spilled over into outright war, and with brutal, large-scale atrocities: the internecine struggles of the Peloponnesian Wars. The effect of this long and utterly destructive war was to devastate Athens, make poverty commonplace throughout the Peloponnese, and replace an Athenian domination with a Spartan one. Athens was humbled, and subsumed within the Spartan

political system. The War was recounted by Thucydides (c.460–400 BC), an Athenian general turned historian, who fought in the conflict, in his *History of the Peloponnesian War*.

Greek philosophy, meanwhile, was taking great strides forward. The enigmatic Socrates (c.470–399 BC) exerted great influence in the Athens of his time—and thereafter. He was studied by Islamic scholars in the 8th century AD, played an important role in the Italian Renaissance, and was admired by Kierkegaard and Nietzsche. Socrates is universally acknowledged as the founder of Western philosophy. His most well-known student was the young Plato (428–348 BC), who also became a pivotal figure in the history of philosophy. His *Republic*, written around 375 BC, is one of the most influential and persuasive works of political philosophic argument, set during the background of the Peloponnesian War, and in the form of a Socratic dialogue on Justice in a utopian city-state where the philosopher is king. Plato's student was the third member of the great triumvirate: Aristotle, who joined Plato's Academy in Athens at the age of seventeen. Aristotle was a polymath, and his thoughts on logic, ethics, rhetoric, political science, and the scientific method, had a profound effect on the early thinkers of both Islam and Christian faiths, and his influence on logic persisted up to the 19th century. After Plato died, Aristotle accepted the invitation of Philip II of Macedon to tutor his son, the young Alexander—the future Alexander the Great.

By the 4th century BC astrology had become a central feature of Greek culture, and was essential for a fuller understanding of religion, science and politics in the ancient Greek world. Astrology in ancient Greece was a diverse series of practices built on the idea that the stars, planets and other celestial phenomena possess significance and meaning for events on earth. It assumed a link between the earth and the skies in which all existence—spiritual, psychological, and physical—is interconnected. It became attached to the schools of Plato, Aristotle, and the Stoics.

* In the ancient world, the terms "astrology" and "astronomy" were essentially interchangeable. The practices only began to diverge after the invention of the telescope. (Variously attributed to Dutch eye glass maker Hans Lippershey and his near neighbor Zacharaias Jansen in 1608. In 1609 Galileo heard of the Dutch "perspective glasses" and promptly devised his own.)

THE HELLENISTIC PERIOD 323 TO 30 BC

The final great age of ancient Greece was the Hellenistic Period. It is the story of how the Armies of Alexander the Great, the famous martial leader of the Greek kingdom of Macedonia, crushed the Persian Empire. He created a much bigger one for Greece that stretched from southern France, Spain, Sicily and the kingdoms of Italy to the west, to Asia Minor/Anatolia, Egypt, and all the way to the western coast of India and Afghanistan. He became the Egyptian Pharaoh in 332 BC, and in 331BC, Alexander founded a major Egyptian city, Alexandria. After his untimely death in 323 BC, Greek control of Egypt passed to Ptolemy I Soter, who had been the Macedonian administrator under Alexander.

The Ptolemies ruled Egypt for almost 300 years, until 30 BC. They made Egypt one of the wealthiest countries in the Mediterranean: as well as carrying out many successful irrigation and land reclamation projects, they shifted Egypt's capital to Alexandria. This only served to increase Greek Hellenistic influence on Egyptian art and culture. There was much assimilation and syncretisation of ancient Egyptian religious ideas with the Greek Religion during this time, and Greek values generally predominated across much of the Mediterranean region.

In the 3rd century BC the Great Library of Alexandria was established, dedicated to the Muses, the inspirational goddesses of the arts, literature and science. The Library was one of the most important centers of learning in the ancient world. Its chief librarian was the Greek polymath Eratosthenes (c.276–c.195 BC), who desired to know all the complexities of the entire world. He is the first person known to have divined, and calculated, that the Earth is not flat, that it is a globe, and that furthermore, it has an axial tilt. He then proceeded to calculate its circumference. He devised a calendar of 365 days to one year, and that every fourth year there would be 366 days.

After the defeat of the Greek armies by the Roman empire at the battle of Corinth in 146 BC, Rome's influence in the Mediterranean grew inexorably. The definitive Roman occupation of the Greek world was established after the Battle of Actium in 31 BC, when Augustus defeated Cleopatra VII, the Greek Ptolemaic Queen of Egypt, and her lover the Roman general Mark Antony. In 30 BC Octavian took the Egyptian capital of Alexandria - by then the last great city of Hellenistic Greece. From thenceforward, ancient Greece became absorbed within the ever-growing Roman empire.

TOP: Marble bust of Alexander the Great. A Roman copy circa 3rd–2nd century BC.

ABOVE: Roman mosaic of Alexander the Great with his horse Bucephalus at the battle of Isus.

BELOW: Alexander and Porus by Charles Le Brun, painted 1673.

1

GREEK MYTHOLOGY

Since civilization began, societies have used myths, legends, and gods, to explain the unexplainable. The Greeks were no exception.

TOP: A marble statue of Eirene (Peace), holding Plutus (Wealth) in her arms. This is a Roman copy after an original Greek statue which stood on the agora in Athens, circa 370 BC.

ABOVE: Early 19 century brooch shows King Priam of Troy on his knees begging Achilles for the body of his son Hector, as told in Homer's Iliad.

They used their mythology to explain and understand their environment, the natural phenomena they bore witness to, and the passage of time and seasons. Through Greek myths, they were able to explain the communicate their religious beliefs, the origin and lives of their gods, as well as humanity's beginnings, and where they would go when they died.

Greek myths humanized their gods, as well as giving advice on how humans should lead their lives, so that it was a happy and prosperous one. Some myths were also used to retell events in history so that it would not be forgotten, and people could continue their connection with their ancestors, as well as the new discoveries and lands and wars fought by various adventurers.

The term 'myth' may imply a lack of authenticity, or something that should not be believed under any circumstances, but it is impossible to say to what degree the Greeks wholeheartedly believed their stories, or knew that they were embellishments to explain the unexplainable. It is likely that every story was believed by some and discarded by others, as is the case with every religious story. It is entirely possible that some of these myths' only purpose was entertainment.

What we do know is that Greek society clung to their myths, and that they were both familiar and popular with most of the population. We can see this in their art, whether it's a painted piece of pottery, a sculpture, or one of the many grand buildings still standing to this day.

When mythology would have first begun spreading, stories and myths were passed on almost entirely by word of mouth, most likely by Minoan and Mycenaean bards from the

18th Century BCE and onward. This means that the myth could be changed depending on the speaker, embellished or improved to entertain a new audience, or simply edited due to the orator's internal bias. However it is also possible that no such changes occurred, as an attentive audience might have argued changes from story to story, and there may have been certain rules about what kind of changes could be made to a story without agreement.

The first written versions of myths were in a series of poems by Homer and Hesiod around the 8th Century BC. Homer focused mostly on grand epic tales of heroes, famously recounted the Iliad and the Odyssey, whereas Hesiod's Theogony focused on the lineage of the gods, and his Works and Days describes the creation of man. The gods are described with human feelings and failings, and heroes are created, often with one divine parent and one mortal.

After writing, myths began being presented through pottery from the 8th Century BC onward. This would have allowed audiences who couldn't read and didn't have time to sit and listen to stories for hours on end access to the same myths, thus spreading the mythology to a wider audience.

Greek mythology remained popular for many years, with large sculptures decorating buildings such as the Parthenon at Athens, the Temple of Zeus at Olympia, and the Temple to Apollo at Delphi representing scenes from mythology. In the 5th Century BC, theatre became yet another form of spreading the myths, and around the same time began the first documented skepticism of the myths, with the rise of philosophers who desired more scientific answers to all of life's great questions.

In the 5th century BC, Herodotus and

Thucydides documented a less subjective view of events as accurately as they were able, to keep on record.

In general, the Greeks created myths that reflected elements of the human condition, by humanizing these creatures so above themselves and giving them the same flaws as humans. Their creation myth has two sons usurping their fathers, referring to the struggle between family members and generations. The Titanomachy represents the defeat of chaotic elements and the subsequent proper order of things.

The Greeks even created gods of Fate and Destiny, and frequently told stories of the gods interfering with humans lives, either favorably or not, perhaps wrestling with the notion of free will and choice. The gods also showed that wrongdoing would be punished, that medicine and music are divine gifts, and that abstract concepts could be made concrete, as in Justice (Dike), Peace (Eirene), and Lawfulness (Eunomia).

For the Greeks, Heroes represent traits and deeds to aspire to – bravery, strength, perseverance. Other mythological characters, such as King Midas, warned of the consequences of greed, or Narcissus of vanity, or otherwise bad behavior to be avoided. The Greeks used their mythos to explain natural occurrences, such as Persephone's journey to the Underworld heralding winter, or the passage of the sun being driven by Helios, or even Time itself. Their creatures represent chaos, destruction, lack of reason – things to be overcome by the heroic characters, and ultimately bested in pursuit of purity and prosperity. They symbolized overcoming difficult tasks, like cutting off one hundred Hydra heads. They represented faraway exotic lands and piqued the imagination, such as the three-headed dog Cerberos who guarded Hades.

Just as stories continue to do to this day, myths could also be used to explain unfamiliar experiences. One could imagine that King Minos' grand, sprawling palace was like a

labyrinth if a humble Greek had never been there before. And perhaps Jason's expedition for the Golden Fleece was merely a way of retelling the Greek expedition to plunder Caucasus for all of its gold? Were the Amazons truly a tribe of only women, or was it simply a culture where women were treated more equally? Are Sirens meant to warn foolhardy wanderers away from unfamiliar territory?

Myths are not just fanciful stories, true or not: they are morality tales, they are warning signs, and they are fanciful spins on true events. One thing is for certain: every day more archeological finds have been added to a growing body of evidence that says the traditions and stories from Greek mythology had an origin and a purpose.

ORIGINS

The functions of myths are not just to answer the basic questions of 'Where do we go when we die?' and 'Who made the first people?', but it was to also justify and explain the existing social system, and account for traditional rites and customs.

In Ancient Greece, stories about gods, goddesses, heroes, and monsters were an important part of everyday life. There is no single text that has every myth and legend. The earliest were told by word of mouth and spoken stories, and don't usually introduce the gods and goddesses of the time, as they would have been so integral to the day to day lives of those telling and listening to them.

Around 700BC, Hesiod wrote the Theogony, which was the first written and documented origin story in Greek mythology. It depicted the universe's journey from nothingness (Chaos, the void), to existing, with a wide and elaborate family tree which contained everything. Elements, personified phenomena, and even the Underworld were all given names, rulers, and roles in this collection.

OPPOSITE: Inlaid wood showing Chaos with arms outstretched and one eye looking at the void, and watching the start of creation.

CHAOS

In the absence of all else, Chaos reigned.

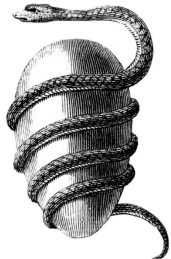

TOP: Ovid born 43 BC. One of the greatest poets ranked with Virgil and Horace and extremely popular during in his lifetime.

ABOVE: The Cosmic Egg is found in many cultures and civilzations. The egg symbolizes the unification of two complementary principles (the yolk and the egg white), from which all life emerges.

ABOVE RIGHT: Nyx (Night) and her children Aither and Hemera.

Chaos, which translates into 'The Gaping Void' in Ancient Greek, was perceived as the origin of everything, the empty, unfathomable void from which every other god and goddess emerged.

Chaos was first described as a mass of energy and darkness, full of random disorder, that existed in the emptiness that was before the creation of the universe. Later, Chaos formed a Cosmic Egg in its belly, which hatched the first deities into existence.

Chaos was often personified as female, though the placement and tangible qualities of Chaos changed between different poets and historians. Some, most notably Hesiod, believed

that Chaos was a physical place, that was dark and gloomy and buried far underground, while others thought Chaos was a space that sat between the Earth and the Sky. The Roman poet Ovid, who described Chaos as being the source of all the elements, built upon Chaos' original mythology and furthered the female assignment in later myths.

The first deities that emerged from the Cosmic Egg formed within Chaos were Gaia (The Earth), Tartarus (The Underworld), Eros (Love), Erebus (Darkness), and Nyx (Night).

TARTARUS

Tartarus is described in Greek mythology as being both a primordial deity, third to exist after Chaos and Gaia, and a physical place.

TOP: Two headed Orthrus being calmed by Heracles. The tree between them represents the sacred grove of Persephone, wife of Hades.

ABOVE: Greek urn showing Persephone supervising Sisyphus in the underworld.

OPPOSITE TOP: Tantalus condemned to be unable to eat or drink for eternity.

OPPOSITE BOTTOM: Elysium and Tartarus. The State of Final Retribution. James Barry mural.

Some descriptions of the location call it a dark, deep abyss, a dungeon of torment – essentially, the Ancient Greek version of Hell, as opposed to the Underworld, which was where souls went after they died and didn't have any traditionally negative implications.

Tartarus is more traditionally described as a place instead of the deity, although he did conceive Typhon with Gaia. Typhon was a giant serpent monster who once challenged Zeus for his title, and after a violent battle, was imprisoned in Tartarus along with other titans. They were eventually freed by Zeus, when he waged war against Cronus and the other titans, for the right to rule Olympus. After Zeus won, Cronus and his allies were then imprisoned in Tartarus.

Tartarus also conceived, with Gaia, Echidna – the Mother of All Monsters – and Typhoeus – the Father of All Monsters. Echidna and Typhoeus would go on to conceive creatures such as Cerberus, The Hydra, The Nemean Lion, The Chimera, The Sphinx, and The Caucasian Eagle.

Since Tartarus was the pit of eternal punishment, it seems only fitting that Tartarus the deity was the one responsible for carrying the souls of sinners to Tartarus after their judgement. Tartarus was even deeper underground than the Underworld, approximately nine days down from Earth.

Some notable residents of Tartarus, among their children and enemies that the gods feared would overthrow them, were mortals guilty of some truly atrocious acts against the gods. King Sisyphus not only considered himself a peer of the gods, but violated the laws of hospitality, and tricked the god of death when Sisyphus was meant to be punished, thereby temporarily stalling death itself. Sisyphus was sentenced to roll a heavy boulder to the top of a slope, but the boulder would never make it to the peak, and would always roll back down.

King Tantalus cut up his son, boiled him, and served him for dinner when the gods invited him to dine with them. He stole secret ambrosia of the gods, and lied to the gods when his friend stole a golden dog forged by Hephaestus. His punishment was to stand in a pool of water beneath a fruit tree. If he tried to reach for the fruit, the branches would rise and prevent him from eating. If he tried to bend down and drink, the water receded, so he was forever starving and dying of thirst.

There were three judges who determined if a soul would be sentenced to Tartarus, outside of the punishment of the gods. Rhadamanthus judged Asian souls, Aeacus judged European souls and Minos judged Greek souls. If they decided that the souls presented to them for judgement were unjust, they would be sentenced to Tartarus.

In some myths, Tartarus shares a purpose with Catholic Purgatory. Tartarus was a place of purification through suffering – those who had

committed crimes which were 'curable' could be purified there, and in theory earn a chance to leave and go to the Underworld for the rest of eternity. Those that were deemed 'incurable' were eternally damned, giving Tartarus its secondary purpose: a place for punishment and torment, the equivalent of Hell for Ancient Greeks.

Of course, Ancient Greek philosophers would regularly debate over what was deemed a curable or incurable offense. Plato believed that temple robbers and murderers were incurable, but if someone had committed involuntary manslaughter, or murdered someone but regretted it for the rest of their lives, they were allowed to leave Tartarus after one year and ask forgiveness of their victim. If they were forgiven, then they were redeemed. If they were not forgiven, they would be damned to Tartarus forever.

Before the world came into existence, the Greeks had Chaos. After an immeasurable amount of time, the elements began to consolidate and form themselves into two different substances. The lighter section rose high and formed a sky or firmament, a vast arching vault over the firmer, solid mass underneath.

GAIA AND URANUS

These two masses were Uranus and Gaia. Uranus was the more refined deity, representing heaven and light, purity, and omnipresence. Gaia, beneath him, was the nourishing mother earth.

Gaia was universally worshipped by the Greeks, and almost every city had a temple in her honor. Her name was invoked during every solemn oath, declaration, or plea for assistance among the Greeks. Quickly after their formation, Uranus married Gaia, and their union was reflected on the earth. Heaven's light bloomed flowers, and Gaia quickly birthed Oceanus as water on her surface to nourish life on earth. Uranus also produced Aether, which was the atmosphere above Gaia that only immortals could breathe, and then Aër (Air), which could be breathed by mortals. Between these siblings were the Nephelae, the restless sister clouds. Gaia produced mountains and the sea, and united herself with the sea, creating Nereus, Thaumas, Phorcys, Ceto, and Eurybia.

Erebus (Darkness) and Nyx (Night) also emerged from Chaos at the same time, and with Uranus, Nyx created Eos (Aurora), the Dawn,

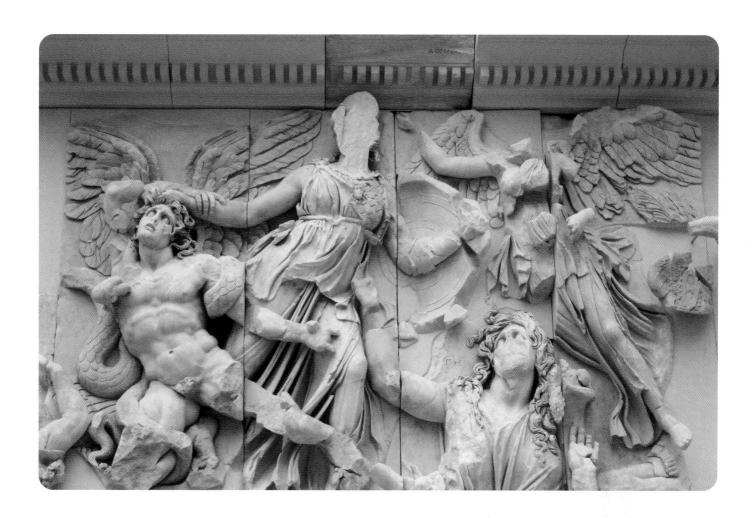

and Hemera, the Daylight. In addition to these children, Uranus and Gaia produced the Giants and the Titans.

The Giants were made of two types, the Cyclopes and the Hecatonchires. The Hecatonchires each possessed one hundred hands and fifty heads, and along with the Cyclopes were giant creatures known for their brute strength, who created earthquakes and volcanoes with their massive, strong bodies.

There were twelve Titans in total: Oceanus, Ceos, Crios, Hyperion, Iapetus, Cronus, Theia, Rhea, Themis, Mnemosyne, Phoebe, and Tethys.

Uranus hated the Giants for how crude, rough, and turbulent they were, and feared that the great strength of his children may one day overwhelm him and harm him.

He ended up throwing the Titans into Tartarus, which served as a dungeon for immortal beings, and sealing the Giants inside of Gaia's womb. This prompted Gaia to enact a plan of revenge against Uranus for the crime of imprisoning and harming her children. She conspired with her son Cronus to harm Uranus and free the rest of his siblings.

ABOVE: Frieze in marble and limestone showing the battle between gods and giants. Athena holds Alcyoneus by the hair while Gaia looks up in horror.

OPPOSITE: Mosiac showing Uranus in a sphere decorated with signs of the zodiac, looking down on Gaia and her children who represent the four seasons.

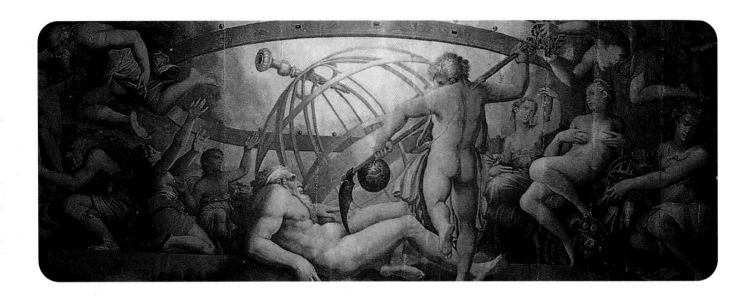

CRONUS' REBELLION

ABOVE: The mutilation of Uranus by Cronus, painting from the ceiling of Palazzo Vecchio in Florence, Italy.

OPPOSITE: Saturn devouring his son. The three stars above them represent the planet Saturn. Rubens 1636.

> **CRONUS** The youngest Titan, son of Gaia and Uranus.
>
> Often depicted as an older man carrying a sickle, scythe, or a warped sword.
>
> Famously appears in art as a thin old man devouring his living child.

Cronus was the youngest of Gaia and Uranus' children, and became the leader of the first generation of Titans. Fueled by fear of being overthrown or harmed by his children, Uranus sealed Cronus and his siblings inside of Gaia and in Tartarus, which prompted Gaia to plead with her children to rise up and do something about Uranus. She was too full of grief and anger to allow Uranus' abuse of her children to continue.

Cronus was the only child unafraid to take action against his father. Gaia created an adamantine sickle and hid it on a mountain, for Cronus to use when Uranus' guard was down. Cronus escaped his prison and slipped up to the mountain. When Uranus descended to consort with Gaia, Cronus seized the sickle and castrated his father. He hurled away Uranus' severed genitals, where they rolled into the sea, and produced a white foam that spawned Aphrodite. The blood from Uranus also fell to the earth and created Gigantes, Meliae, and the Furies (Erinyes).

Uranus cursed Cronus to suffer the same fate he had – that one day, one of Cronus' children would rise up and overthrow him, just as Cronus had done to Uranus. Then, wounded and defeated, Uranus fled and faded into obscurity, leaving an empty throne and Cronus more than willing to fill it. Cronus freed his Titan siblings as he had promised Gaia, but kept the Giants imprisoned in Tartarus. The Titans became the power in the universe, and Cronus married his sister Rhea.

Cronus' reign began as one that was mighty and prosperous. Free from her grief and burden, Gaia went on to fertilize the land, and the 'Golden Age' for humans and gods alike began. There was no immorality, and no need for laws because no one wronged each other. The world flourished under Gaia's happiness.

Many attribute Cronus' association with harvest and agriculture to this prosperous time.

CRONUS AND RHEA

Despite this peaceful time, Uranus' curse plagued Cronus, and he became tyrannical and paranoid, obsessed with the idea that one of his children would rise up against him and usurp him, possibly in the same humiliating and violent way that he had usurped Uranus.

Driven by his incessant fear, Cronus began to devour every child he had with Rhea, sure that if he killed them all and didn't allow them to grow to adulthood, they would not be able to rise up against him. Rhea gave birth to Hestia, Demeter, Hera, Hades, Poseidon, and Zeus in that order, and Cronus swallowed all except Zeus.

Rhea was not happy with the loss of her children, and so when Rhea was pregnant with Zeus, she went to Gaia to ask for help. Gaia told her to go to Crete and give birth in secret. Zeus was born in Crete and hidden away from Cronus. Rhea gave him a stone wrapped in swaddling clothes, which the Titan swallowed, having been successfully tricked.

Rhea hid Zeus away in a cave on Mount Ida, where he grew up well-guarded and nursed by a mother goat named Amalthea and the Meliae, until he was old enough to rise up against his father, free his siblings, and end Cronus' tyranny.

OPPOSITE: Rhea tricks Chronus into swallowing a stone in place of Zeus.

LEFT: Marble statue of Rhea, daughter of the earth goddess Gaia.

33

IAPETUS, HYPERION, AND THEIA

Iapetus was one of the titans, the son of Uranus and Gaia. He was the titan of mortality, craftsmanship, and one of the four pillars who held up the sky – he was the western pillar.

With the Oceanid Clymene, he fathered Prometheus (the titan of forethought), Epimetheus (the titan of an afterthought), Atlas (the titan of strength), and Menoetius (the titan of violent anger).

In some tales, Iapetus was the titan who presided over a mortal lifespan, and determined and assigned mortal creatures their mortality and finite existence. He was one of the gods, along with his brothers Coeus, Crius, Hyperion, and Cronus, who oversaw time itself. He had a reputation for being one of the more destructive titans, who helped restrain Uranus while Cronus castrated him. Homer wrote that Iapetus sat with Cronus in Tartarus after Zeus' rebellion.

Other iterations refer to Iapetus as the piercer, and the god of violent death. He is often depicted as wielding a spear and bringing painful death to those whose lives are due to end. However, this piercer nickname could have been referring to his title as the god of craftsmanship, and that the spear was a tool, not a weapon.

LEFT: Hyperion god of wisdom and light.

Iapetus' sons were supposed to embody humanity's worst traits. Even Prometheus, the benefactor of mankind, taught them how to be sneaky and deceptive. Epimetheus was foolish and never thought ahead. Atlas was too daring, and witless. Menoetius was too angry and reckless. Due to these traits being passed to mankind, Iapetus is regarded as the grandfather of mankind, and the one responsible for man's more dubious natures.

Hyperion is the titan god of heavenly light, another son of Uranus and Gaia. He is one of the 12 Titans of Greek Mythology and said to be 'God of watchfulness, Wisdom, and the Light'. Prior to the Olympian gods, Hyperion was the physical incarnation of the sun. He shone the brightest of all Uranus' and Gaia's children.

Unfortunately, very little is known about him, and he is not featured heavily in any surviving mythology. When referred to, he is only labeled 'father of the lights and heaven' and said to be glorious and shining, but not much else. In some versions of the Uranus castration myth, Hyperion joined his brother Iapetus in holding Uranus down so that Cronus could castrate him.

The later Ancient Greeks interpreted Hyperion as being the literal father of the light, and therefore the father of Helios, the god of the sun, Eos, the dawn, and Selene, the moon. Hyperion is another of the four pillars that hold up the cosmos. With his influence over his children, Hyperion was viewed as a primal god who had control of the day-night cycle, since the sun, moon, and dawn were his children and therefore obedient to him.

One story is that Hyperion is the one who gifted mankind with eyes and sight, since the Ancient Greeks believed that the eyes emitted light and that this was surely a gift from Hyperion. This also supported his title as the watcher and would explain why he would give humanity the same ability.

What little else we know about Hyperion suggests that he was on the side of Cronus during Zeus' rebellion, and that his sister-wife and mother of his children was Theia. Theia was a titan goddess of 'shining elements'. She was associated with shining metals, jewels, and light. The Ancient Greeks believed that her eyes emitted beams of light and that she was the goddess of sight. She was also associated with the gift of prophecy. She is sometimes credited with giving man the gift of sight.

Theia is always depicted as an incredibly beautiful, striking woman, with long hair and flowy clothing that shows the light around her. She is either directing light towards the earth, or moon, or holding it in her hands. In some depictions she is shown to be with child. Her most consistent feature is her eyes, which always shine with beams of light, and often have the sun and moon in them to reflect her children.

ABOVE: Atlas holds up the world.

LEFT: A bust of Menoetius, the titan of violent anger.

BELOW: Part of a frieze showing Theia, titan goddess of shining elements.

THE BIRTH OF ZEUS

After Cronus overthrew his father Uranus, having been convinced to do so by his mother Gaia, he ruled over the Titans with his sister and wife, Rhea. However, Cronus soon developed a reputation for being power-hungry, tyrannical, and most of all, paranoid.

Uranus had cursed Cronus at the moment of his attack, saying that just as Cronus had risen up against his father, so too would one of Cronus' children rise up and overthrow him from the throne, and be greater and stronger than Cronus ever was.

Being of completely sound mind, Cronus decided the best way to avoid this was to eat his children. He ate all the children Rhea bore him, until Rhea was pregnant with Zeus. She fed Cronus a giant stone that she had wrapped in swaddling blankets, and secreted her newborn son away on the Isle of Crete, with the help of Gaia, to keep him hidden. Special demons named 'Curetes' would beat their shields so that Cronus didn't hear the baby crying.

On Crete, Zeus was raised by nymphs and fed milk and honey with the help of Amaltheia, a mother goat. Her broken horn was how the nymphs managed to nurse him until Zeus was old enough to eat solid food. As Zeus grew up, he became strong enough to rise against his father as the prophecy foretold.

First, he took a herb given to him by Gaia, and gave it to Cronus, promising that it would give him immeasurable power. Instead, it made Cronus very sick – sick enough to vomit up all of Zeus' siblings, and the stone he'd swallowed instead of Zeus.

Zeus then allied with his siblings, and freed the Cyclopes and Hecatonchires from Tartarus, where they had been imprisoned, to join him in the fight against Cronus and the rest of the Titans. Thus began the Titanomachy, the formative war for the Olympian Pantheon.

OPPOSITE: The cave where Zeus was born in Crete.

BELOW: The Battle Between the Gods and the Titans. Joachim Wtewael 1600.

THE TITANOMACHY

The Titanomachy, also known as the Battle of the Gods, War of the Titans, or just The Titan War, refers to a ten-year period during which the Olympian Gods fought for dominance of the universe with the gods who lived on Mount Othrys.

Cronus and Gaia set in motion events which led to a war between Zeus and his siblings. This also involved the older Titan gods. Uranus, who was the sky and ruler of the cosmos imprisoned the Hecatonchires and Cyclopes in Gaia's womb. She in turn convinced their children, known as the Titans, to castrate Uranus.

Though she had 12 children by Uranus at this point, only Cronus agreed to assist his mother. Gaia gave Cronus access to an adamantine sickle she had forged and hidden away on Mount Othrys. When Uranus arrived at the mountain to consort with Gaia, Cronus ambushed him and castrated him with the sickle. He cast the genitals of Uranus across the Mediterranean. From the blood that fell on the earth, three sets of children were born; the Gigantes, the Erinyes, and the Meliae; while from the blood that fell into the sea, the goddess Aphrodite was born. Cronus then used the sickle to open Gaia's womb and free the imprisoned Hecatonchires and Cyclopes.

Cronus imprisoned the Hecatonchires and Cyclopes in Tartarus, along with his newly-castrated father Uranus. Cronus then became leader of the Titans. Angered by this betrayal, Uranus cursed Cronus so that the children of Cronus would one day rebel against him, just as Cronus had rebelled against Uranus.

Cronus became the new cosmic ruler, but because of the curse of Uranus, he was so paranoid about being overthrown that he quickly became a similar kind of tyrant, and would devour all of the children he fathered with his sister-wife, Rhea.

Rhea, similarly to Gaia, began to resent Cronus for eating her children, and when she bore Zeus, she hid Zeus away from Cronus so that he wouldn't be devoured. She instead tricked Cronus into eating a magnetite rock wrapped in a blanket, which had been given to her by Gaia.

Rhea brought Zeus to Crete, where he was raised in a cave by a mother goat named

The Fall of the Titans, painted by Cornelis Cornelisz between 1596-1598. It shows the ferocity of the ten years of battles between the Titans and the Olympians. The war was fought to decide who would have dominion over the universe.

Amalthea, and a group of nymphs called the Meliae who had been created from the castration of Uranus. When Zeus was old enough, he disguised himself as a cupbearer of Cronus and gave him a mix of mustard and wine, which caused Cronus to vomit up his now-full-grown children.

Now that his siblings were freed, Zeus led them in rebellion against Cronus and the rest of the Titans who had not defected to fight on his side. Hestia, Demeter, Hera, Hades, and Poseidon were his allies and were also gods. Additionally, Zeus freed the Hecatonchires and Cyclopes from Tartarus, where they had been imprisoned by Cronus, and they became his allies as well. The Hecatonchires hurled large stones, and the Cyclopes forged Zeus' thunder and lightning bolts.

The Titans fought on the side of Cronus, with the notable exception of Prometheus and Themis. Atlas was an important leader who fought with Cronus. The war lasted for ten years, with Zeus the eventual victor. He imprisoned the Titans who fought against him, in Tartarus, and made the Hecatonchires their guards. Atlas was then punished by being made to hold up the sky.

In some legends, Zeus freed the Titans when he was secure in his power.

After Zeus and his allies won the war, the world was divided among him and his siblings. Some legends say that the siblings drew straws, while other legends conclude that each brother was given a dominion suited to their natures and proclivities.

Zeus was given dominion of the sky and air, and became the ruler of the gods. Poseidon became lord of the sea and all the waters, and Hades was given dominion of the Underworld. The earth was left without specific ruling which allowed the gods to do as they pleased.

2

THE GODS

THE GODS

At the center of Greek mythology is the pantheon of deities who were said to live on Mount Olympus, the highest mountain in Greece, from the time of the Titanomachy onward.

These gods ruled every aspect of human life on their tall mountain, and while their predecessors were either monsters or incorporeal beings like 'The Sky', these gods and goddesses were more human in appearance. They were also susceptible to human emotions such as jealousy, and capable of erring.

The original new gods were: Zeus, the king of the gods and god of thunder and lightning; Hera, the queen of the gods, the goddess of marriage; Poseidon, god of the sea; Hades, god of the Underworld; Demeter, goddess of agriculture; and Hestia, goddess of the hearth. The Olympian pantheon expanded later to include Apollo, the god of prophecy; Ares, the god of war; Athena, the goddess of wisdom; Aphrodite, goddess of love and beauty; Dionysus, the god of wine; Hephaestus, the smith of the gods and god of fire; Eros, god of physical love; and Hermes, the messenger god.

When Zeus ascended to the throne after overthrowing Cronus, he divided the world into three parts and gave a domain each to his brothers, Poseidon and Hades. Each god took a piece that was suited to their temperament – Zeus remained in the clouds and ruled the sky, Poseidon ruled the tempestuous ocean, which could either be friendly or deadly, and Hades ruled the dark and quiet Underworld, removed from the affairs of the living.

The remaining gods were granted domains based on their unique traits. The Earth, however, was to remain independent of a single ruler.

Distant view of Mount Olympus, the highest mountain of Greece and home of the ancient Greek gods.

Zeus was the last child of Cronus and Rhea, and the one who freed all his siblings from his father's stomach before waging a war against the ruling Titan.

ZEUS

TOP: Zeus and Hera on Mount Ida

ABOVE: Zeus holds his thunderbolt above his head ready to strike.

OPPOSITE: Zeus disguised as a swan in love with Leda.

This resulted in his victory and eventual rule over Mount Olympus and the world below. As the god of justice he was frequently called on in myths to settle disputes, decide competitions, and work out conflicts among the other gods. Despite his numerous affairs outside of marriage with Hera his sister and wife, Zeus was an honorable character who helped or hindered many heroes as he saw fit.

Zeus wasn't just king of the gods, he was related to pretty much all of them. If he wasn't someone's brother, he was a lover, or a father. Hera was not the first wife of Zeus – he had married Metis, the Titaness of wise counsel. However, when he found that she would bear a son more powerful than him – he swallowed Metis when she was pregnant, and ended up giving birth to Athena from his own skull. Athena grew inside the head of Zeus until his headache was crippling, and he asked Hephaestus to crack his skull open. When he did, Athena burst forth, fully formed and armed, and became the goddess of Wisdom and the tactical side of war. She is generally considered to be the favorite child of Zeus.

Zeus then married Themis, the Titaness of Justice. She gave birth to the Three Fates, after which Zeus ended the marriage, since the Fates were already powerful enough and he feared that she would give him an even more powerful child.

Zeus then married Eurynome, and they created the three Graces.

Hera was the last wife of Zeus, his elder and beautiful sister. He was faithful to her for a time, but quickly began to turn his sights elsewhere, much to her grief and anger. It was the dalliances of Zeus that usually caused trouble for mortals, he would sire monsters or legendary heroes, and Hera would be close behind to exact revenge on whoever Zeus had wooed.

One such mortal was a woman named Semele who had become pregnant by Zeus. Hera found out and disguised herself as an old woman. She befriended Semele who confessed that she was pregnant by Zeus. Hera, persuaded Semele to ask Zeus to show himself in his full glory to prove that he was really the god he claimed to be.

Hera then left, and Semele asked Zeus to grant her one wish. Zeus swore on the River Styx that he would give her whatever she desired. When she asked to see him in his full glory, Zeus begged her to reconsider, but she would not be swayed. Semele didn't know that seeing a god or goddess in their true form was too much for a mortal, and would cause them to burst into flames.

Semele fatally insisted that Zeus prove himself. Zeus gathered the ashes of Semele's body and saved their son, Dionysus. Hermes took Dionysus to be raised by a band of Maenads, and grew up to invent wine, which made Zeus so proud that he granted Dionysus immortality and allowed him to live on Olympus.

One of the earliest myths of non-traditional animal combinations is that of Zeus and Europa. She was a Phoenician princess, daughter of King Agenor of Sidon. One day, Europa woke from a strange and troubling dream, and invited her companions, all daughters of nobility, to join her in gathering flowers by the sea.

Zeus saw them and noticed Europa in particular, she was by far the most beautiful. Zeus went to the group and appeared as a large gentle white bull, smelling of wildflowers. The maidens were so taken with the bull that they all rushed up to pet him. Zeus bided his time, until Europa approached, and laid down for her to climb on his back. Once she did, he charged off into the sea and swam away. They were joined by a procession of nymphs, and Triton, the first merman, and Poseidon himself. Europa

realized that the bull must be a god and became afraid, pleading for the gods to pity her.

Zeus was quick to assure her that this abrupt kidnapping was an act of love. He took her to Crete and promised her that she would be safe, and would bear him many sons. Europa became the mother of Minos and Rhadamanthus, among others.

At least Zeus kept his word – Hera never found out about this particular affair, so Europa and her children were safe from the vengeful queen.

Another example of Zeus turning into an animal to have his way with a mortal woman is the story of Leda and the swan. Leda was a princess, daughter of the king of Aetolia. When she was old enough she married Tyndareus of Sparta.

Zeus saw Leda and fell in love with her. He took the form of a swan to appear and sleep with her. She slept with her husband on the same night, and from that night produced two eggs, inside each was a set of twins. The first set was Helen and Clytemnestra; and the other was Castor and Pollux. Versions of the myth are not

ZEUS King of the Olympians, god of the Sky, Weather, Thunder, Lightning, Wind, Clouds, Law, Order, Justice, Power, and Human Fate. He is called 'The Father of the Gods'.

His most prominent symbols are the eagle, the thunderbolt, the bull, and the oak.

Portrayed as an incredibly strong man, with a thick beard, clothed in fine robes with a severe expression.

TOP: Large terracotta of Zeus abducting Ganymede.

ABOVE: Apollo, Zeus and Hera. Calyx crater 420-400 BC.

OPPOSITE: The wedding of Zeus and Hera painted on to a wall in Pompeii.

consistent and it is unclear which children were the those of Zeus and which those of Tyndareus. All myths agree that Pollux was immortal, and that Helen was the daughter of Zeus.

While it's true that most of the stories of male gods and their lovers center around beautiful young women, there are many stories with male love interests. Perhaps the most famous one is between Zeus and Ganymede.

Ganymede was a prince of Troy, renowned for being exceptionally beautiful. He was said to be the most beautiful human on earth, male or female. While Ganymede was tending sheep, Zeus caught sight of him. Zeus turned himself into a giant eagle and flew down, abducting the boy and carrying him to Olympus to be cupbearer of the gods.

While this story doesn't explicitly say that he and Zeus were lovers, it's generally accepted that their relationship was a romantic one, especially since Zeus compensated Ganymede's father with some immortal horses, in the same way a dowry might be exchanged. Ganymede is also often depicted with a rooster, which was a traditional gift between lovers in Greece.

Despite being male and therefore unable to sire children, Hera was jealous of Zeus' favor for the prince. To keep him safe, Zeus placed Ganymede as a constellation in the sky – he

became Aquarius, the Water-Bearer, and sat next to Aquila, the Eagle, so that they would always be associated with each other. Zeus also covered Troy in a heavy cloud during its fall, so that Ganymede wouldn't have to see the city he once called home, go up in flames.

While Zeus was the god of justice, and the king of the Olympians he frequently made mistakes. A significant one, at least from the perspective of a mortal, was sending down Pandora and giving her a box full of misery, disease, hatred, and all the bad aspects of human life – and the curiosity to want to open the box.

It had started as a revenge plot against Prometheus for stealing fire from the gods to give to man, since Prometheus had created mankind and loved them so much. Zeus wanted to punish them, so he sent Pandora. The problem was misery and disease were things which grew quickly and spread fast. Soon, humanity was so corrupt that it became a problem.

Zeus decided to create a great flood and drown everyone. The only exceptions were King Deucalion, son of Prometheus and who was considered the most honest man on earth, and his wife Pyrrha. They survived the flood on a giant boat and went on to repopulate the earth.

Hera was the youngest daughter of Cronus and Rhea, and their third child overall.

HERA

HERA Daughter of Cronus and Rhea, sister to Zeus, Poseidon, Hades, Demeter, and Hestia.

Goddess of marriage, associated with family and the welfare of women and children.

According to some, Hera's name is not her actual name, merely the translation of the word 'Lady' or 'Mistress', according to her title as Queen of the gods.

Normally portrayed alongside Zeus as an older, beautiful, matronly woman with a crown, or wreath, and a veil. Sometimes she carries a scepter topped with a pomegranate and a cuckoo, which symbolizes fertility, and the method Zeus used to 'woo' her. She is also often accompanied by a peacock, which is one of her sacred animals.

She was one of the siblings to be swallowed by Cronus and then vomited up when Zeus freed them. Some say that technically Hera is the oldest daughter since they were vomited up in the reverse order of being eaten.

Zeus chased Hera with the intention of lying with and marrying her, but she evaded him until he tricked her. Knowing how much she loved animals, he turned himself into a cuckoo in distress. His cries drew Hera to him, and when she lifted him to her breast to keep him warm, Zeus transformed into his real self and assaulted her. She was so ashamed of being tricked and taken advantage of that she agreed to marry him.

Hera gave Zeus four children: Ares, the god of War; Eileithyia, the goddess of childbirth; Hebe, the goddess of eternal youth; and Hephaestus, the god of fire.

Despite Hera being beautiful, she didn't have much choice but to be faithful to Zeus. She was the guardian of marriage and the King's spouse, and therefore no other god, nor many mortals, would lay a hand on her. The few who tried were met with swift vengeance – Endymion was condemned to an eternal sleep, and Ixion, a mortal man who had been invited to live on Olympus, was tricked by Zeus into making love with a cloud that looked like Hera. Thereafter

Ixion was bound by Hermes to a wheel of fire that never stopped spinning.

While Zeus wasn't faithful, he was certainly a creative hypocrite. For a long while, Zeus was a brutal and a cruel leader, lording over his Kingship with unmitigated, tyrannical behavior. Hera quickly grew tired of this treatment and plotted to rebel against him. With Poseidon, her brother and god of the sea, as her ally, as well as Athena and potentially a few other gods – Zeus had plenty of disgruntled family members to choose from.

Hera drugged Zeus and bound him to his bed. Her allies helped her, and stole his thunderbolt. Thetis, however, summoned Briareus, who untied the prisoner. Zeus was freed and tormented Hera for her treachery by hanging her from the sky with golden chains. Hera vowed to never rebel again if she was allowed to be released, and so she was forced to direct her anger at Zeus towards his lovers and offspring. This quickly added to her reputation as a jealous and vengeful goddess.

One example was with Semele as related in the section on Zeus. She was a princess of Thebes, daughter of Cadmus, a famous Greek hero, and Harmonia. Zeus fell in love with Semele after witnessing her sacrificing a bull on his altar and visited her often, soon making her pregnant

Zeus saved the unborn child and sewed it into his thigh, eventually giving 'birth' to Dionysus. Dionysus would later save his mother from the Underworld and bring her to Mount Olympus, where she became the goddess Thyone.

Another example of Hera's vengeance was when she turned Callisto into a bear after Callisto gave birth to Arcas, a child of Zeus. Arcas was a great hunter and after some time, he was hunting Callisto and attempted to kill her as a bear. Zeus saved Callisto by taking both her and Arcas and placing them in the sky, where they became the constellations Ursa Major and Ursa Minor – the Big and Little Bear.

Io was perhaps the lover who suffered the most for her dalliance with Zeus. Zeus turned her into a cow in an attempt to hide her from Hera, then Hera sent Argus Panoptes to watch her, which prompted Zeus to send Hermes to kill Argus. Hera turned the ghost of Argus into a gadfly, which bothered poor Io all the way to Egypt. Zeus eventually impregnated her with Epaphus.

Hera was not fond of nymphs, either, since these curious and beautiful sprites were the frequent and flirty companions of Zeus and would often partake in affairs with him. One such nymph, Echo, tricked Hera by leading her on a wandering journey through the forest so that Zeus and the other nymphs had time to hide and get away from Hera's rampage. Echo was very chatty and thorough in her

ABOVE: Bronze figures of Zeus on his throne with Hera at his side.

OPPOSITE: Ancient theatre in Delos. Site of birth of Apollo.

modesty and was said to be very beautiful.

Zeus was enamored by her beauty, and instead of letting his marriage to Hera stop him, he pursued a relationship with Leto. She was eventually seduced by him and became pregnant.

Hera once again found out, and promptly set a course to stop Leto from ever giving birth to her child. She warned all land and water not to give Leto sanctuary, and covered the earth in cloud so that Eileithyia, the goddess of childbirth, wouldn't know that her services were required.

Hera also tasked the Python to pursue Leto relentlessly so that Leto was not able to rest and recover from her labor pains. Leto eventually came to Delos, an island which agreed to give her sanctuary if Leto promised to transform it into a great island afterwards.

Since Delos was not specifically considered land or water, it wasn't breaking Hera's oath by offering refuge to the poor Titan. However, when Leto touched Delos, it became connected to the ocean floor so that it no longer floated, and was transformed into an island paradise.

In some versions Delos was considered to be the transformed version of Asteria, Leto's sister, who had become this shape to escape the lustful advances of Zeus in previous years

Leto was finally safe and gave birth to Artemis, the goddess of the hunt. Artemis was said to help Leto give birth to her own twin, but the baby's birth was delayed for nine days and nights. Eventually Eileithyia discovered that Leto was in need and arrived on Delos, where Leto finally gave birth to Apollo.

Hera's penchant for vengeance wasn't just in matters of the dalliances of Zeus. Hera was just as vain as her husband, considering herself the greatest and most beautiful, since she was the Queen. Orion's wife Side boasted that she was just as beautiful, a mistaken claim, as Hera sent her to the Underworld. When Antigone made the same mistake, Hera turned her into a stork.

Despite having been promised power and glory from Hera if Paris chose her. He chose Aphrodite as the most beautiful of goddesses, thus making Hera a sworn enemy of Troy.

distractions. Once Hera realized she was being delayed and tricked on purpose, she cursed Echo, only to be able to repeat the last few words someone said, back to them.

Nymphs and mortals weren't the only ones charmed by Zeus. Leto was one of the Titans to be allowed to live freely after the rebellion of Zeus and the Titanomachy, since she had not taken sides during the war. She was the cousin of Zeus, as her parents and the parents of Zeus parents were siblings. Prior to the reign of Zeus, she was the goddess of motherhood and

POSEIDON

Poseidon was the second son of Cronus and Rhea, and the brother of Zeus, Hades, and the rest of the first generation of Olympian gods.

POSEIDON Son of Cronus and Rhea. Named God of the Sea after the rebellion of Zeus .

Often depicted as an old man, carrying a trident and surrounded by waves.

A very moody god, either extremely friendly and cooperative, or prone to bouts of mass destruction, much like the sea itself.

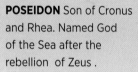

ABOVE: Marble statue of Poseidon, in his right hand he would have originally been holding a trident – said to be fashioned by the three Cyclopes.

Poseidon was swallowed by Cronus along with his siblings, and then vomited up when Zeus freed them all. After Zeus' rebellion, Poseidon was given dominion over the oceans.

Poseidon's myths and behavior are just as varied as the seas themselves – he shared Zeus' penchant for ill-advised dalliances, and would offer assistance to those who prayed to him. One such person was King Minos, who had the famous minotaur problem during his reign.

Minos was given the Cretan Bull by Poseidon, which was the pure white bull formed from the sea. This bull was a sign from the gods that Minos was the true ruler of Crete, which was a subject of question among his brothers and subjects. He was meant to sacrifice the bull to Poseidon, but decided to keep it for himself. This prompted Poseidon to seek punishment.

He turned the docile and beautiful Cretan Bull into a raging beast, making it go completely wild and destroying everything in its path. Then, Poseidon asked Eros to make Pasiphae, the wife of Minos , fall madly in love with the wild bull. Eros did so, and Pasiphae was consumed by uncontrollable lust for the bull.

She commanded Daedalus, a great inventor who served Minos, to construct a hollow wooden cow that Pasiphae could climb into and be made love to by the bull. Pasiphae became pregnant with the minotaur through this union.

That wasn't Poseidon's only involvement with animals. While he wasn't known for turning himself into animals and seducing human woman, he did relentlessly pursue his sister Demeter, who transformed herself into a mare to escape his advances. She hid among the horses of King Onkios, but Poseidon realised that she was not a normal animal. He turned himself into a stallion, caught her, and mated with her. From this Demeter gave birth to Arion, who was a horse that was capable of human speech. While Poseidon had many lovers, mortal and immortal, male and female, he also had a wife – Amphitrite, a goddess of the seas, springs, and aquatic life. She was the daughter of Oceanus and Tethys, and Queen of the Seas. With Poseidon she bore Triton, Rhode, and Benthesicyme.

ABOVE: Pasiphae wife of King Minos in love with the pure white bull. Gustave Moreau.

LEFT: Poseidon with his wife Amphitrite riding through the waves, pulled by four horses. While he is God of the sea, she is Queen of the seas.

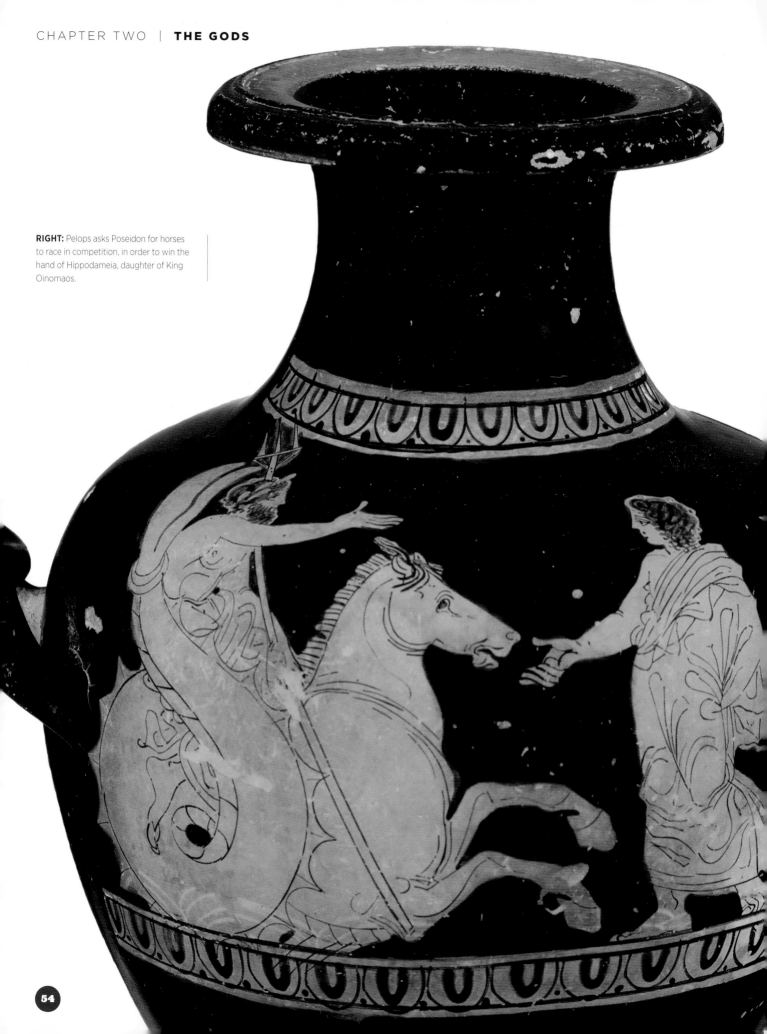

RIGHT: Pelops asks Poseidon for horses to race in competition, in order to win the hand of Hippodameia, daughter of King Oinomaos.

Poseidon first saw her when Amphitrite was dancing with her sisters and decided he wanted her. Amphitrite ran from him, but Poseidon was persistent, and summoned the dolphin king Delphinus to find Amphitrite and persuade her to marry Poseidon.

Delphinus was a lovely creature, and managed to persuade Amphitrite to listen to him. He told her that her steady nature would calm Poseidon's volatile one, and there would be harmony and joy in the sea if they were married. Poseidon placed an image of Delphinus in the sky as a reward for his service.

It wasn't long after their marriage that Poseidon went back to his extramarital affairs and bouts of violence. Amphitrite was getting annoyed and jealous, particularly with Poseidon's increasing obsession with the sea nymph Scylla. In a fit of jealousy, she threw herbs into Scylla's bath, which transformed her into a terrible and hideous monster, with twelve arms and six mouths.

As God of the sea, Poseidon played a part in the Trojan War, though his involvement started a lot earlier. Sometime before Troy began, Zeus' wife, Hera, had grown tired of her husband's arrogance and anger, so plotted a revolt against him. Poseidon and Apollo were some of her allies in this, so when they failed, Zeus saw fit to punish them.

He temporarily stripped them of their divine abilities and powers, and sent them to King Laomedon of Troy, who made them build giant walls around Troy. For payment, he promised each of them some of his immortal horses, but refused payment when the walls were built.

Before the Trojan War, as punishment for not paying his promised reward, Poseidon sent a giant sea monster to attack Troy. This monster was later killed by Heracles. Poseidon went on to support the Greeks during the Trojan war, keeping the ocean calm for their fleets as they set sail to and from the city.

BELOW: Marble frieze showing wedding of Poseidon and Amphitrite.

HADES

As a reclusive and withdrawn individual, mostly keeping company with the souls in the Underworld, Hades doesn't feature much in Ancient Greek mythology.

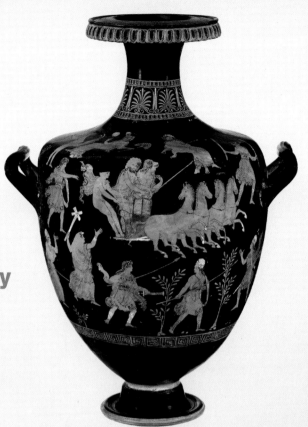

HADES Son of Cronus and Rhea, brother to Zeus and Poseidon, Hestia, Hera, and Demeter.

Given the Underworld as his domain after the rebellion of Zeus.

Rarely depicted in art, but is occasionally shown as a tall, awe-inspiring man with a long beard, wearing a heavy black robe, and with a solemn face. He frequently wears a helmet which grants invisibility, and has Cerberus, the three-headed dog that guards the gates of the Underworld, beside him. His weapon is a two-pronged fork similar to Poseidon's trident.

A nickname for Hades was Plouton, the 'wealth-giver', since precious gems are found underground.

His most notable involvement is the abduction of his wife Persephone to the Underworld. Persephone was the daughter of Demeter, the goddess of agriculture and fertility. Persephone was out gathering flowers with her maiden friends, Hades was on one of his rare trips above ground. He fell in love with Persephone and wanted to make her his wife. In an attempt to lure her closer, Hades caused an incredibly beautiful flower, the Narcissus flower, to bloom in front of her. When Persephone reached out to pick the flower, the ground opened up and Hades appeared in his chariot, and ferried her away to the Underworld.

Demeter was so distressed at the sudden disappearance of her beloved daughter that she wandered aimlessly in search of her, causing a great famine to spread throughout the land. In her sorrow she neglected her duties of keeping the earth warm for the crops and helping them grow. Finally, Hecate and Helios told her what had happened, and Demeter left Olympus to search for Persephone.

This caused the earth to become completely barren, and after a year passed, the gods began to worry that Demeter's absence would cause all of humanity to die out for lack of food. Zeus started sending all the gods out with offerings and promises in an attempt to bring Demeter

back, but all Demeter wanted was Persephone.

Knowing this, Zeus sent Hermes down to Hades to request Persephone's return. Hades agreed, but Persephone had eaten four pomegranate seeds while in the Underworld, which bound her to this realm forever. Zeus decided on a compromise; Persephone would spend four months with Hades, and the other eight above ground with her mother.

This now corresponds to the winter and summer months – while Persephone is above ground, Demeter is happy and brings life to the earth, and when Persephone returns to the Underworld, Demeter abandons her post on Olympus and grieves for the four months, causing winter.

Another myth that includes Hades is largely conflated with Thanatos, the god of death. King Sisyphus of Corinth was ruthless and frequently violated the rules of hospitality and generosity meant to be offered to travelers and guests. Zeus kidnapped the daughter of Asopus and Sisyphus revealed her whereabouts. Zeus was furious and decided to punish Sisyphus. He asked Thanatos, god of death, to take Sisyphus and chain him up in the Underworld. When Thanatos went to Sisyphus, the king asked how the chains worked, and contrived to chain up Thanatos in his place.

Now that there was no one to welcome the dead into the Underworld, thousands of souls were wandering mindlessly on the banks of the River Styx. In different versions of this myth, one has Thanatos being freed by Ares who was frustrated that no one was dying in his wars. In another it is Hades who has been chained, and the gods have threatened Sisyphus with great reprisals if he doesn't free Hades.

In another myth, mortals Theseus and Pirithous, went to Hades on an apparent binge of wine-induced heroics. They tried to kidnap Persephone, wife of Hades, from the Underworld. The two men were on their merry way through the Underworld, but never made it to Persephone.

They stopped at a rock to rest, only to realize that they were unable to stand. They were suddenly pursued by the Furies who were ready to torment them with terrifying screeches. Heracles managed to free Theseus, but Pirithous wasn't so fortunate. When Heracles tried to free him, the ground started shaking so violently, he was unable to be freed. Hades kept him in the Underworld as punishment for his hubris in trying to kidnap the wife of a god.

THIS PAGE: Sisyphus, king of Ephyra, condemned by Zeus to push a large boulder uphill, which continuously fell to the bottom.

OPPOSITE: Terracotta water jar, circa 340-330 BC. It shows the abduction of Persephone by Hades surrounded by gods and deities.

Mars and Venus surprised by Vulcan, painted
by Alexandre-Charles Guillemot 1827.

APHRODITE

Aphrodite was a goddess known for her incredible beauty. Her most common creation myth is that she was born from the foam of the sea waters off Cyprus after the genitals of Uranus were cast into the water by Cronus.

Aphrodite was often sympathetic towards star-crossed lovers, or injured relationships. As the goddess of love, often passionate and unwise love, she frequently starred in myths where two people were united against all odds.

She was known to be especially vain because of her looks. She was shallow, valuing beauty above all else, and detested ugliness. She had the ability to make anyone fall in love with anyone, including Zeus, and had tremendous power over lust and carnal desire. She was considered perfect, and is usually seen wearing luxurious silks, jewels, and a crown or diadem encrusted with precious gems.

Aphrodite was also a nurturing and protective goddess, both of lovers and of her own family. She turned Ino into a bird to escape Hera's wrath after an affair with Zeus, and gave beauty to Orion's daughter after the death of her mother. She also took care of the orphaned daughters of Pandareus. He had been turned to stone by Zeus after trying to steal from the temple.

She was fond of making unions for people. Pygmalion was a famous sculptor and King of Cyprus, who fell in love with a statue that represented his ideal of womanhood. Since he could not find the perfect woman, he swore to celibacy, but was plagued by this love for a statue that could not return it. Pitying him, Aphrodite turned the statue into a living woman, who married Pygmalion and gave birth to Paphos.

Zeus, the king of the gods, feared that because she was so beautiful, other gods would fight over the right to be her husband and that it would cause upset. To avoid this, he arranged for Aphrodite and Hephaestus, the god of fire and the forge, to marry each other.

That is one version. The second is that Hephaestus was angry at his mother, Hera, for making him so deformed and ugly, so he created a magic throne that bound her in place when she sat on it. In return for her release, Hephaestus was given Aphrodite's hand in marriage.

It is considered that Aphrodite didn't have much of a say in it, and to marry the most beautiful goddess to a god that was notoriously ugly and deformed was certainly a bold choice.

APHRODITE Cronus cast the genitals of the castrated Uranus into the sea from which Aphrodite was born of the sea foam. In some versions of her myth she is the daughter of Thalassa (the sea) and Uranus, and sometimes she is the daughter of Dione the Titaness, and Zeus.

Goddess of love, lust, passion, desire, beauty, sex, pleasure, and procreation.

Often associated with passionate, usually ill-advised love, incredibly beautiful, and usually portrayed coming out of the sea fully formed, standing on an open shell.

Hephaestus was happy with his marriage, and created beautiful jewelry, including a golden belt which made her look even more irresistible. Aphrodite wasn't so easily won over and had frequent affairs with both gods and mortals. She and Ares had a long affair. The sun god Helios spied them in the middle of the hall of Hephaestus, and immediately informed Hephaestus.

Hephaestus wanted to catch them in the act, so he fashioned a special diamond net that was impossible to see, to catch the couple in bed together. When it was time, he threw the net, trapped Ares and Aphrodite in a passionate embrace. Hephaestus wanted to further humiliate them, so he invited all the other gods to bear witness to it. They were mocked for being so foolish, and fled once they were freed – Ares, to Thrace, and Aphrodite to Cyprus.

Far from learning her lesson, Aphrodite continued to have many torrid affairs, her lovers included Poseidon, Hermes, and Dionysus. She didn't only have affairs with gods, however. Aphrodite was accidentally struck by one of the arrows of Eros, and fell in love with Adonis. Adonis was killed by a boar, and went to the Underworld, which was the domain of Hades and Persephone.

Aphrodite journeyed to the Underworld and asked Persephone to raise him until she returned, and Persephone agreed. However, during the time in the Underworld, Persephone also fell in love with him, and refused to return him when Aphrodite came back. They were unable to agree who should have him, so went to Zeus to decide. Zeus declared that Adonis would split his time above and below ground to be with the two of them – four months with Persephone, four months with Aphrodite, and four months with whomever he wanted.

BELOW: Venus and Anchises. William Blake Richmond.

OPPOSITE LEFT: The legendary rock of Aphrodite on the island of Cyprus.

OPPOSITE RIGHT: Bronze statue of the beautiful Aphrodite holding the golden apple.

Adonis favored Aphrodite, and Persephone was so jealous that she arranged for another boar to chase and kill him. He died in Aphrodite's arms.

Another famous mortal lover of Aphrodite was Anchises, a Prince of Troy. Some stories say Zeus made her fall in love with him as punishment for making other gods fall in love with mortal women. Aphrodite disguised herself as a Phrygian princess and seduced Anchises, making love to him in disguise so that he didn't know she was a goddess. She revealed herself nine months later when she gave him their son. Aphrodite warned him not to brag that he had lain with a goddess, because Zeus would strike him down. Anchises did, unfortunately, and was crippled by a thunderbolt from Zeus.

The goddess of discord threw a golden apple, which was said to belong to the fairest, into a circle of three goddesses. Hera, Athena and Aphrodite were unable to agree as to which of them was the fairest and most gifted, and turned to Zeus for a judgement. He was unable to make a decision between his wife, daughter and aunt and asked the mortal Paris to make a decision. Hera offered power, Athena offered military might and wisdom, and Aphrodite offered the heart of the most beautiful woman in the world. Paris chose Aphrodite, who gave him the love of Helen of Sparta with whom he eloped, thereby causing the Trojan War.

After the sack of Troy, Homer's Iliad tells that Aeneas carried his elderly father out of the burning city to safety. Aphrodite guided her son to the place where eventually Rome would be built. This gave Aphrodite the title Guardian of Rome by poets such as Virgil.

Leto, Apollo's mother, was a female Titan who drew the lustful attention of the Greek God Zeus. They had an affair and Leto became pregnant, with Hera finding out soon after.

APOLLO

APOLLO Son of Zeus and Leto.

The God of the sun, light, music and poetry, healing, prophecy and knowledge, order and beauty, archery and agriculture. Meant to be harmony, reason, and moderation personified, both physically superior and morally virtuous.

Statues of him depict a tall, beardless, athletic man wearing a laurel crown and carrying either a bow and arrow, or a lyre and plectrum, The tripod symbolizing his prophetic powers was usually near him in art, and he is linked with the wolf, dolphin, python, mouse, deer, and swan.

Also known as 'Phoebus', meaning 'bright', 'Loxias, the one who speaks crookedly', and 'Leader of the Muses'.

Hera sent Python after Leto, and Python chased Leto all over the world while Leto was in labor, forbidding the earth or any islands from giving the Titaness rest or relief from her labor pains.

The island of Delos, which was technically neither island nor a land mass, accepted Leto and gave her a safe place to give birth to her first child, Artemis. Artemis then helped Leto deliver Apollo nine days later.

Nursed with nectar and ambrosia, Apollo soon grew strong, and within four days was set on a quest for revenge against those who had mistreated his mother and had tried to prevent the birth of him and his sister. He went to Parnassus, where Python lived, and shot the monster with many arrows. Python managed to escape that attack, taking shelter in the sanctuary of Gaia at Delphi.

Apollo was so furious at Python that he violated the sanctuary and attacked, staining it with Python's blood. For reparations, Apollo was ordered by Zeus to cleanse himself, which he did, before returning to Delphi to claim the shrine in his own name.

Delphi and Delos became sacred sites for Zeus, Leto, Artemis, and Apollo's worshippers. Pythia, who was a high priestess over the Temple of Apollo, became the enigmatic oracle of Delphi, and played a significant role in many myths thereafter.

The god Hermes stole the cattle of Apollo on the day of Apollo's birth. By way of reparation, Hermes offered Apollo a lyre which he had just created. This became the most common symbol to be associated with Apollo.

Apollo's brilliance and skill were unmatched, but there were those who attempted to challenge him. The satyr Marsyas was one such unfortunate creature. He played the double flute, also called the aulos, at which he was very skilled – some would say he rivaled Apollo. However, he was unable to play and sing at the same time, unlike the god, and so he ultimately lost the contest. As punishment for his hubris, Marsyas was hanged inside a cave and flayed alive.

Pan was another satyr who challenged Apollo, though he survived the encounter. He challenged Apollo on his pan flute, but lost the contest by an almost unanimous vote. Only King Midas thought that Pan was the better player. Apollo was so insulted that he gave Midas a pair of donkey's ears in return, as he obviously lacked a human ear's ability to appreciate music in the first place.

Another challenger was the King of Cyprus, Cinyras. He played the flute, but he also lost to Apollo. Depending on the version of the story, Apollo either killed him, or he committed suicide from shame.

ABOVE: Musical duel between Apollo and Pan in which Apollo was the victor.

LEFT: Marble statue of Leto, with her children Artemis and Apollo.

LEFT: White marble statue of Apollo.

Apollo was a well-loved god by both men and women, mortal and immortal. Often he loved them back just as deeply. The more famous stories of his love affairs are the ones that are the most tragic.

Daphne was the most famous of Apollo's ill-fated loves. She was a nymph, and had vowed to the goddess Artemis that she would remain innocent for her entire life. Apollo fell for Daphne and chased her, persistent and relentless as most Greek gods were. Finally, Daphne was unable to keep up the chase, so she prayed to the river god Peneus to turn her into something else, so that she could remain innocent. When Apollo rushed to embrace her, she was transformed into a laurel tree. Apollo swore that he would love Daphne forever, and wore a laurel wreath in remembrance of her.

Another famous affair was that of Apollo and Cassandra. Cassandra was a Trojan princess, and Apollo wished to earn her favor. He offered her the gift of prophecy if she would to sleep with him. She agreed and Apollo gave her the gift of prophecy, but when she reneged on the agreement he cursed her. Thereafter her prophecies would be entirely accurate, but no one would ever believe her, no matter how hard she tried to convince people.

Some other notable would-be lovers feature in myths as well. Coronis was Apollo's current lover, and she was pregnant with his son Asclepius, when she fell in love with Ischys and began an affair with him. A white crow told Apollo of this, and Apollo was so enraged that he told Artemis to kill Coronis. He also burned the feathers of the messenger crow, which is why all crows are black.

Apollo also had the misfortune of falling in love with a married woman, Marpessa. Her husband Idas had already gone through many trials for her, risking his own life to be with her. When Apollo tried to fight for Marpessa, Idas threatened him with a bow, not caring that he was a god. Zeus ended up having to intervene and asked Marpessa to choose. She chose Idas, since he was mortal, and she was afraid Apollo would not love her when she grew old.

Like Daphne, both of Apollo's most well-known and beloved male lovers were turned into plants. Cyparissus accidently killed the pet deer which he had been given by Apollo. He asked Apollo to make him sorrowful forever, so Apollo reluctantly turned Cyparissus into a cypress tree.

Hyacinthus was a favored lover of Apollo, and he loved Apollo in return. Zephyrus, the West Wind, was insanely jealous of this love, as he also loved Hyacinthus. Zephyrus contrived to have Hyacinthus hit by his own discus when he and Apollo were practising together in a field. Apollo created a flower out of his spilled blood, which became the Hyacinth flower.

Though Apollo was divine and meant to be one of the more virtuous gods, he was not without failings. After killing Delphyne, Zeus commanded Apollo to serve under a mortal, and Apollo chose Admetus, who was the King of Pherae (part of Thessaly), and who would later become one of the Argonauts. He was a fair and just king, and made Apollo his herdsman.

Later, after his years of service, Apollo helped Admetus win the love of Alcestis, princess of Iolcus, daughter

LEFT: Apollo chasing the nymph Daphne. She was unable to keep up the chase, so she prayed to the river god Peneus to turn her into something else, so that she could remain innocent. When Apollo rushed to embrace her, she was transformed into a laurel tree. This statue show her hair changing into leaves of the laurel.

of Pelias. Admetus won by being the victor in a competition, the task was to yoke a boar and a lion to a chariot. Apollo helped Admetus in this task, and therefore the King was able to win the hand of Alcestis for marriage.

When the Fates determined the death of Admetus, Apollo got them drunk and persuaded them to allow him to live, if someone else took his place. Alcestis agreed to take the place of Admetus in the Underworld, and was escorted down by Thanatos, the god of death.

Later, after Heracles had completed his Twelve Labors, Admetus was kind to him, and so Heracles repaid him by going to the Underworld and retrieving Alcestis, allowing her to rejoin her husband in the land of the living.

That was an example of Apollo's kindness and servitude. During the Trojan War, Apollo's story is one of wrath and vengeance. While Apollo's actions may appear to be somewhat removed from the actual War, they were instrumental in the progression and eventual conclusion of the War.

Apollo was not just the master of the lyre and a skilled hunter. He was also the god of coming of age, and his rituals were performed by young males as they sought to become men of the community, with various roles and responsibilities as a full citizen. These rituals included tests of strength and prowess.

Apollo was also known as the vengeful god of plagues. These two things are related.

Apollo was a proud god, who would bring about swift and immediate punishment to those who had offended him and his family. Nine years into the Trojan War, Agamemnon and Achilles raided the town of Lyrnessus, killing Chryseis as a prize. Chryseis was the daughter of one of Apollo's priestesses, and was given to Agamemnon, while princess Briseis of Lyrnessus was given to Achilles.

Chryseis' father begged Agamemnon to return her, offering a ransom, but Agamemnon was a proud man and thought Chryseis was a better prize than his own wife. Chryseis'

father then turned to Apollo for help, making sacrifices and praying to him to get his daughter back. Apollo answered the man's pleas, sending a plague upon the Greek army that killed its horses, cattle, and eventually made its way to the soldiers. Agamemnon was eventually forced to give up Chryseis and returned her to her father.

Agamemnon, demanded that Achilles give him Briseis as consolation. Achilles was furious at the command, but obeyed it, afterwards withdrawing from the fighting and refusing to help the Greek forces. He took many of his men with him which, for a long time, provided a huge drop in Greek efficacy against Troy's defenses.

Apollo further assisted Troy under the order of Zeus. After Achilles left the battlefield, Apollo and Iris were sent to assist. They knocked down many of the Achaean fortifications, giving Troy a huge advantage, and Apollo filled Hector with enough strength to face down Ajax and lead the Trojan army onward.

Patroclus was the dearest friend of Achilles, and when the Greeks were losing the war, Hector took up arms and eventually killed Patroclus. Achilles was so saddened by the death of his friend that he rejoined the war, marking the beginning of the end for Troy.

TOP: Marsyas, who lost the contest to play his flute and sing against Apollo. His punishment was to be hanged and flayed alive. See page 62.

ABOVE: Admetus, the victor in a competition, the task was to yoke a boar and a lion to a chariot. Apollo helped Admetus in this task, and therefore the King of Pherae was able to win the hand of Alcestis for marriage.

OPPOSITE: Menelaus, king of Sparta and younger son of Atreus, carrying the body of Patroclus who had been killed by Hector in the Trojan war.

Behind them a Roman statue of a woman.

ABOVE: A 16th century bronze medal with Helen of Sparta.

OPPOSITE: Paris and Helen, painted by Jacques Louis David, 1788.

BELOW: Watercolor painting of the panorama view on the Islands of Delos, the birthplace of Artemis and Apollo.

Apollo was one of the gods who actually intervened within the war, outside of random acts of divine intervention that affected seas and wind. He sided with Aphrodite over Athena and Hera during the debate about the golden apple, and subsequently supported Paris and his reward, which was Helen of Sparta, given to him by Aphrodite.

Since Aphrodite championed Paris, so too did Apollo. After the death of Patroclus, Zeus knew that Achilles' grief would lead to the complete decimation of Troy, and so he permitted the gods to interfere as they saw fit. While most agreed to sit back and watch, Apollo decided to act. He convinced Aeneas to battle Achilles first, which would have proven a losing battle had Poseidon not intervened and swept Aeneas away. Hector then stepped up to face the mighty Greek, but Apollo convinced him to turn away from the fight. Hector was Troy's strongest soldier and they couldn't afford to lose him.

Eventually, Hector was killed by Achilles, meaning Paris had to take up arms against him. It was said that, being both a skilled archer and knowing Achilles' only weakness, Apollo guided the arrow of Paris to strike Achilles' heel, finally leading to his death.

ARES

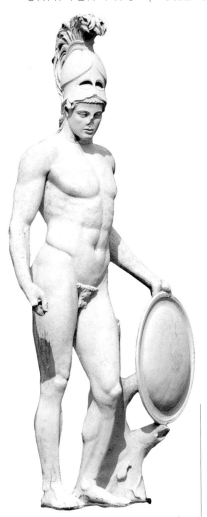

ABOVE RIGHT: 5th century BC bronze statue of Ares.

ABOVE: Marble statue of Ares carrying his shield and wearing a helmet.

OPPOSITE: Wall painting of Ares and Aphrodite, found at Pompeii.

Ares was one of Zeus and Hera's children, along with Eris, the goddess of discord, and Enyo, the goddess of destruction.

ARES God of War. Other names include 'the bane of mortals', 'the slayer of men', 'the city-stormer', 'the armor-clattering'.

Son of Zeus and Hera, and one of Zeus' least-favorite children.

Usually represented wearing a helmet, carrying a shield and either a sword or a spear.

He drives a four-horse chariot and is accompanied by dogs or vultures.

It's no surprise that Zeus and Hera produced such chaotic and recklessly destructive children, given the nature of their relationship, and Ares was no exception.

Although Ares was the only son Hera gave Zeus, Zeus was never fond of him, and there are stories which suggest that Zeus would have banished Ares to Tartarus were it not for the fact that Ares was his son.

Because Zeus was so dismissive and thought so badly of Ares, the other gods had no reason to show him favor either. Many of myths of Ares involve him either suffering some sort of humiliation, or performing some ill-thought and recklessly destructive act and having to deal with the consequences.

While Ares was the god of war, he was not the same as Athena, the goddess of war. Athena was favorite child of Zeus and represented the tactical and reasonable side of war, with planning, forethought, and logic. Ares was purely about the destructive parts of war, the violence and brutality of fighting and death.

Ares is rarely alone on the battlefield. He usually comes with a hoard of bloodthirsty denizens that symbolize the terror and chaos of his side of the war. Deimos (Panic) and Phobos (Fear) are two of his sons often by his side. Eris (Discord) and Enyo (Destruction and 'Sister of War') are frequent comrades for Ares as well.

Other members of his troupe include Kydoimos, who personifies the confusion in the midst of battle, and the Keres, who are the female spirits of death and dress in blood-stained cloaks.

As Ares was known to be a savage god, who relished senseless violence, he was almost universally detested. He was often wounded in battle and would run to his father to complain. During the Trojan War Athena mocked him, showing that she was a superior warrior.

Ares didn't just lose to gods; he was defeated in battle by Heracles as well. Otus and Ephialtes, the Aloeadae, managed to capture Ares and keep him in a bronze jar for thirteen months. If Hermes hadn't been told about it, he likely would have stayed there forever.

One of the exceptions to being public enemy number one was Ares' love for Aphrodite. She was his lover for a long time, even during her marriage to Hephaestus, who caught them in a net during one of their liaisons. Yet another story where the humiliation of Ares takes center stage.

Aphrodite bore Ares as many as eight children, depending on which myths you read. Phobos, and Harmonia are the certain three, and later their children include Adrestia and some or all of the four Erotes: Eros, Anteros, Pothos, and Himeros.

Another of Ares' known lovers was Eos, the

Titan goddess of the dawn, sister of Helios, the sun, and Selene, the moon. She was married to Astraeus, god of the dusk, and had many children with him, before beginning her affair with Ares. Aphrodite caught wind of the affair, and while Eos and Ares had no children together, it was clear that Aphrodite deemed their relationship to be sexual.

She cursed Eos with an insatiable sexual urge, and the ability only to find satisfaction with mortal men. With this curse, Eos abandoned Ares as a lover and abducted several mortal men, including Cephalus, Tithonus, and Orion.

Given the violent nature of Ares, it seems only fitting that he was the first god to stand trial for murder.

Poseidon's son, Halirrhothis, was out one day and came upon Alcippe, who was one of the daughters of Ares. He was consumed by lust and assaulted her. Whether or not he was successful is unclear, though it's largely believed that he only managed the attempt before Ares intervened. Ares heard Alcippe's cries and became so enraged, that he rushed to her side and killed Halirrhothis with his spear.

Poseidon demanded Ares stand trial for murdering his son. Until this point, forcing oneself upon a mortal was pretty commonplace among the gods, so the fact that Ares intervened and saved his daughter was unusual in the first place.

Ares didn't back down, and stood his ground in defending his daughter, so he agreed to stand trial. The trial was held on top of a rock next to the Acropolis, knows as the Areopagus, or the 'Ares Rock'. This rock would go on to be the site for trials around deliberate homicide in the future.

Ares insisted that his murder of Halirrhothis was just, in defense of his daughter, while Poseidon called him a monstrous murderer and wanted him punished. Despite none of the gods being particularly fond of Ares, he was acquitted and set free.

ARTEMIS

Artemis was one of the most revered goddesses of Ancient Greece. She was the daughter of Zeus and the Titaness.

RIGHT: Artemis, goddess of the hunt, here with a 'golden stag' after Dionysus created a mirage.

ARTEMIS Daughter of Zeus and Leto, older twin sister to Apollo.

Goddess of the hunt, the 'Mistress of Animals', goddess of childbirth, virginity, and protector of young girls.

Often depicted as a huntress carrying a bow and arrows.

Sacred creatures were deer, wolves, and the cypress tree.

Leto, who took refuge on Delos after going into labor and being mercilessly chased by a jealous Hera. Artemis was born first, fully formed, and assisted in the birth of Apollo.

Despite being a virgin goddess, Artemis was once tricked into having a child. She had unwisely offended Hera, Athena, and Aphrodite. Artemis told Athena and Hera that they were not virgin goddesses, because Athena had children, and Hera was the goddess of marriage. She also told Aphrodite that love was not worth the trouble, since it almost always ended in a broken heart.

The goddesses, offended by these comments, plotted revenge on Artemis, using Dionysus, who created a mirage that made every young man look like a golden stag. Soon Artemis was in childbirth, which Hera purposely made very painful for her. Some say that the daughter of Artemis was Haley's comet, others that she is the shadows of the night.

Artemis' childhood is not given in any detail in mythology, except for a story where, having been whipped by Hera at three years old, she climbed into the lap of Zeus and asked for six wishes. She asked to remain a virgin, to have many names that would set her apart from Apollo, to be the Light Bringer, to have a bow,

arrow, and knee-length tunic for hunting, to have 60 sea nymphs, all nine years old, to be her choir, and for twenty Amnisides Nymphs to be her handmaidens, who would watch her dogs while she rested.

She didn't want any city dedicated to her, she wanted to rule over the mountains, and to help women through the pain of childbirth. Artemis believed that the Fates had chosen her to be a midwife, as she had helped Leto to deliver Apollo. All of the companions of Artemis remained virgins, and she fiercely guarded her own chastity. She spent most of her childhood seeking out items for hunting, and captured the six-horned golden deer to pull her chariot.

Having made the choice to remain a virgin meant that Artemis became a target from gods and mortals. She had a long complex friendship with Orion, which in some versions say that he tried to rape her. Others claim that he

ABOVE: Actaeon sees Artemis bathing, she is so outraged by this she turns him into a stag. Notice that antlers have started to grow out of Actaeon's head!

attempted to slay every beast in order to win the heart of the huntress, but that she killed him before he could succeed. In another version of the myth, Hera sent Scorpio to kill Orion, so Zeus placed him in the stars as a constellation near Artemis so that they would always be close together.

Alpheus was a river god who was in love with Artemis, but was unable to win her heart. He decided to capture her. She being suspicious of his motives, covered her face with mud so he wouldn't recognize her when she went to visit him in disguise. In another story, Alphaeus tried to rape Arethusa, an attendant of Artemis.

She transformed her attendant into a sacred spring out of pity.

Another attempted rapist was Bouphagos, the son of the Titan Iapetos. Artemis heard his sinful thoughts and struck him down. Artemis turned Sipriotes into a girl because he saw her bathing.

Actaeon was a great hunter, who was often a hunting companion of Artemis. On one such hunt, he spied Artemis while she was bathing naked in her spring, and attempted to assault her. For this offense, Artemis turned him into a stag, where he was subsequently ripped apart by his own hunting dogs.

The Aloadae were Poseidon's twin sons, Otos and Ephialtes, who became enormous as youths. They were fierce and aggressive hunters, and could not be killed except by each other. They never stopped growing, and boasted that they would soon reach the heavens, where they would kidnap Artemis and Hera and keep them as their wives. The gods were afraid of this happening, but Artemis evaded capture by turning herself into a fine doe and jumping between them. The Aloadae threw their spears at the deer at the same time, missing, and accidentally killed each other.

Artemis not only guarded her own chastity fiercely, but also that of her attendants. Callisto, the daughter of King Lycaon of Arcadia, was one of her attendants, who had also taken a vow of chastity. Zeus appeared to her disguised as Artemis and had his way with her, from whence she conceived a son named Arcas. Hera and Artemis changed her into a bear for the 'sin' of sleeping with Zeus, and her son Arcas almost killed her, but Zeus rescued her at the last minute, and put Callisto into the heavens, where she became Ursa Major, and Arcas became Ursa Minor.

Aura was another virgin goddess, the Greek goddess of breezes and cool air. She was a huntress like Artemis, and proud of her maidenhood. She claimed that the body of Artemis was too womanly to be be a virgin. Artemis was enraged at the doubt and rumor, and asked Nemesis for help in revenge. Nemesis arranged for Aura to be raped by Dionysus, which caused Aura to go mad and become an unhinged, dangerous killer. She had twin sons, one of whom she ate, and the other

one, Iakhos, was saved by Artemis. Iakhos later became one of Demeter's attendants and the leader of Eleusinian Mysteries.

Khione, a princess of Pokis was loved by Hermes and Apollo and boasted that she was prettier than Artemis because she was loved by two gods simultaneously. Proud Artemis was so furious, she rendered Khione mute by shooting off her tongue.

TOP LEFT: Dionysus and Aura, whom he raped and caused to go mad.

ABOVE: A copperplate engraving (1661) showing the constellation Orion.

OPPOSITE: The giants Otos and Ephialtes (Ephialtes on the left) were strong and aggressive, growing by nine fingers every month. See how small the two men on the shore are in comparison.

ATHENA

There are a few versions of the story of Athena's birth. One is that Zeus simply had a severe headache, and asked Hephaestus to split open his skull. The smith of the gods did so, and Athena emerged fully formed.

ATHENA Not born in the classical sense, but emerged from the skull of Zeus fully formed after he had swallowed her pregnant mother, Metis.

Often seen wearing full battle armor, and her associated symbol is the owl.

Goddess of wisdom and war, and one of the favorite children of Zeus.

Another version is that Zeus married Metis, who was described as the 'wisest among gods and mortal men'. Being afraid of the curse of Uranus which said that the children of Zeus would one day rise up against him, he swallowed Athena whole.

A later version states that Metis was not a willing wife, but a victim of Zeus chasing and assaulting her until she became pregnant. She ran away from him, changing form often, but eventually he caught her, impregnated her, and swallowed her.

Regardless of how she got there, Athena sprang fully formed from the head of Zeus after he ordered his skull to be split open. Athena was favored by many of the gods in the Pantheon, and was lauded as the goddess of wisdom, and the civilized side of war involving strategy and planning.

Another name associated with Athena is Pallas. The epithet Pallas can be derived from the Greek words 'to brandish' or 'young woman'. Essentially, Athena was 'the young woman of Athens'. Later, additional myths were created to explain the origin of the name. One claimed Pallas was a childhood friend of Athena's whom she killed during a friendly combat, and so she took on the name of Pallas in her grief. In another version, Pallas was a giant that Athena killed, and wore his skin as a cloak for her victory trophy.

In her temple on the Trojan Acropolis, there is a statue of Athena that is said to have been carved by the goddess in likeness of Pallas. It was said that as long as the statue remained in the city, Troy would never fall. When the Greeks attacked Troy, Cassandra clung to the statue, but she was torn away and dragged to the other prisoners. Athena was so enraged by this violation against her protection that she attacked the Greek fleet with a storm and scattered all the ships which had not been destroyed.

As Athena was the goddess of war, she frequently appeared in many of the Greek hero myths. Specifically, she was associated with myths involving military victory or great combat victory wherein strategy and

wisdom were paramount to success. Athena, represented the civilized side of war, as well as justice and skill. Whereas Ares was known for blood lust and violence.

After Athena's rise to prominence and being lauded as a goddess of good counsel, practical insight, and significant military advantage, she and Poseidon competed for the patronage of Athens. They determined that they would give the Athenians a gift each, and that the king of Athens would decide which gift was better. Poseidon struck the ground with his trident, which opened a saltwater spring. This gave the Athenians access to trade and water, however the water was salty and undrinkable.

Athena gave the Athenians the first domesticated olive tree, which the king favored, and so he declared that she was the patron of Athens. The olive tree provided wood, oil, and food, and soon became the symbol of prosperity.

TOP: An olive tree grows near the ancient Gate of Athena Archegetis in Athens, Greece – the symbol of prosperity.

ABOVE: Pallas Athena standing on a globe, a spear in her left hand, a shield in her right

OPPOSITE: The birth of Athena, emerging fully formed from the head of Zeus.

ABOVE: Jason being regurgitated by the snake who keeps the Golden Fleece (center, hanging on the tree); Athena stands to the right. Red figure cup from Etruria.

BELOW: Heracles and Athena.

Athena often appeared in myths as a helper of heroes, or punisher of miscreants. Athena advised Argos on how to build the ship that would carry Jason and the Argonauts on their journey. She was also said to have guided Perseus on his quest to kill Medusa, and gave him a shining shield he could use to look at the Gorgon's reflection instead of directly at her. She also guided the blade of Perseus when he struck at Medusa so that he could kill her with one strike. Athena assisted Bellerophon with his taming of the winged horse Pegasus.

Athena is perhaps most frequently shown aiding Heracles. She appears in four of the twelve labors, including the slaying of the Nemean Lion, and helping him hold up the sky while Atlas fetched golden apples protected by a dragon. She is also depicted in art as being the one who drove Heracles to Mount Olympus in her chariot, to present him to Zeus once he was worthy of being deified.

When Clytemnestra was murdered and her son, Orestes, fled to Athena's temple, tormented endlessly by the Furies, he begged Athena and her jury to spare him his fate. Athena had the deciding vote when the jury was split. She voted to acquit Orestes, and declared from then on that should a jury ever be tied, the defendant would be acquitted.

Athena also appears in the Odyssey – the cunning of Odysseus quickly won him Athena's favor. For most of the first part of the Odyssey, Athena merely aided him from afar, putting thoughts and ideas in his head and being a protector from a distance. When Odysseus washed up on Nausicaa's island, Athena appeared in person to tell the princess to rescue Odysseus, and played a role in getting him to Ithaca. When Odysseus arrived, Athena appeared to him as a herdsman and lied to him, saying that Penelope, his wife, had remarried and that Odysseus was believed to be dead. Odysseus lied back to her, with a determination and shrewdness that impressed Athena, prompting her to reveal herself and tell Odysseus what he needed to know in order to win back his kingdom after his long absence.

In contrast, Athena also punished those who offended her or desecrated her temple. A lot of her punishments can be seen from many lenses, and appear contradictory at first. Medusa was a Gorgon, but a beautiful one, who was a priestess in Athena's temple. She was raped by Poseidon in the temple who violated her vow of chastity, so Athena transformed her into her monstrous creature we recognize today.

Some might argue that it made no sense to punish the victim for being assaulted in her temple, but other readings suggest that Athena 'punished' Medusa in this way so that she would not have to fear any unwanted advances again.

Another myth begins with Athena bathing in a spring with one of her favorite companions, which was a nymph named Chariclo. Chariclo's son, Tiresias, happened upon them while he was hunting, and saw Athena naked, so she struck him blind to ensure he wouldn't see what man wasn't meant to see again. Chariclo begged Athena to reconsider and cure him. Athena refused, saying she couldn't restore his eyesight, but instead gave Tiresias the gift of prophecy through understanding the language of the birds.

Athena would also punish mortals guilty of hubris. Arachne was a weaving student of Athena, and became so confident and conceited that she challenged Athena to a weaving contest. They each wove scenes; Athena of her great victory against Poseidon, and Arachne of over twenty instances of infidelity among the gods, including Zeus with Leda, Europa, and Danaë.

While Athena admitted that Arachne's work was incredible, she was offended by the subject matter and the girl's behavior. There are a few versions of the myth, one where Arachne promised never to weave again if she lost the contest, another where she hung herself after Athena lost her temper and destroyed her loom. In each case, Athena took pity on her and turned her into a spider, so that she could continue weaving for the rest of her days.

ABOVE: Marble statue of Athena.

BELOW: Achilles dragging the dead body of Hector in front of the gates of Troy.

Athena became involved in the Trojan War because of the Judgement of Paris. All the gods and goddesses where invited to the wedding of Peleus and Thetis, except for the goddess Eris (discord). She was so annoyed by this that she brought a golden apple to the wedding, inscribed with the message 'for the fairest', and threw it between Hera, Athena, and Aphrodite. The three immediately claimed the apple was for them and began arguing about it. They went to Zeus to decide, but he didn't want to favor one goddess over another, and so gave the decision to Paris, a Trojan prince.

All three of the goddesses were beautiful, and Paris was unable to decide, so they each offered him a gift. Hera offered Paris power over Asia and Europe, Athena offered fame and glory in battle, and Aphrodite said that if Paris chose her, she would give him the love and marriage of the most beautiful woman in the world. Paris chose Aphrodite as the rightful owner of the apple, and Aphrodite gave Paris the love of Helen of Troy in return. Because of this rejection, both Hera and Athena sided with the Trojans in the war.

When Achilles was chasing Hector for revenge after the death of Patroclus, Athena appeared to Hector in disguise, tricking him into thinking she was his brother, Deiphobus. She told him to hold his ground, and that they would fight Achilles together. Hector threw his spear at Achilles, missed, and turned to his 'brother' for help, only to find that Athena had disappeared.

Athena aided the hero Diomedes after Achilles fell, allowing him to be an effective warrior in the fight. Athena is often depicted in artistic representations of the war as an unidentified warrior riding on a chariot. Sometimes Diomedes is in the chariot with her. When the Trojan women went to the temple of Athena on the Acropolis to plead her for protection from Diomedes, Athena ignored them.

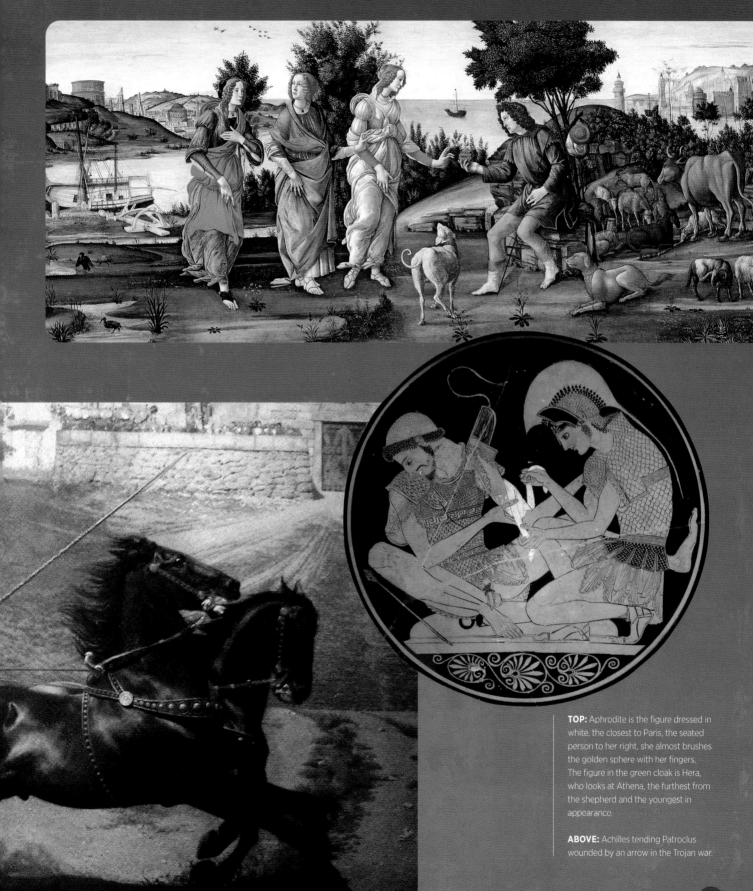

TOP: Aphrodite is the figure dressed in white, the closest to Paris, the seated person to her right, she almost brushes the golden sphere with her fingers. The figure in the green cloak is Hera, who looks at Athena, the furthest from the shepherd and the youngest in appearance.

ABOVE: Achilles tending Patroclus wounded by an arrow in the Trojan war.

Demeter was one of the original six Olympians that were born of Cronus and Rhea, swallowed, and then vomited back up when Zeus freed them all.

DEMETER

DEMETER Daughter of Cronus and Rhea.

Greek goddess of vegetation, harvest, and agriculture.

Mother of Persephone (with Zeus), Plutus, the god of wealth and Philomelus, the god of agriculture and farming (with Iasion, Zeus and the nymph Electra's son), and Arion (with Poseidon).

As the goddess of harvest and growth, Demeter became a central figure to the first Greeks, since she was also given the task of nourishing humanity itself.

The Ancient Greeks believed that Demeter was responsible for the fertility of the earth itself, which meant that if she did not show favor, there would be no crops, and her sorrow would cause a famine. They needed to show Demeter their gratitude so that her wrath or sadness did not affect their food supply.

Demeter had many consorts, and multiple children. Her most famous child is Persephone, the Queen of the Underworld who was abducted by Hades. Demeter was so sad she caused a worldwide famine, until Zeus finally made Hades give Persephone up for some of the year, so that Demeter could be happy. In addition to Persephone, she had a brief liaison with Iasion during the wedding of Cadmus and Harmonia. They disappeared into the countryside together and when they came back, Demeter's dress was covered in mud stains. Zeus saw it and became jealous, killing Iasion immediately with a single lightning bolt. Demeter was already pregnant at this time, and gave birth to the twins Plutus and Philomelus.

One older myth regarding Demeter is that she was once an object of obsession for Poseidon, who chased her, desperately wanting to have sex with her. To escape him, Demeter transformed herself into a mare and hid among a herd of horses, but Poseidon was able to sense her divinity, and turned himself into a stallion so that he could mount her. She bore Poseidon several children this way, including Despoina, the goddess of mysteries (in this version, this is Persephone), and Arion, who was a horse that was capable of human speech.

Demeter was also said to have no fewer than nine children with Triptolemus, who was the son of King Celeus. During Demeter's search for the abducted Persephone, she came across the Palace of Celeus and asked the king for shelter. He agreed, if she nursed his sons, Triptolemus and Demophon.

Demeter agreed, thankful for the rest, and repaid the king's kindness by making the two children immortal. Demeter noticed that Triptolemus was sick and fed him her breast milk. Triptolemus not only recovered his strength but he instantly became an adult.

She then covered Demophon in ambrosia and placed him in the flames of the earth, which would burn the boy's mortality away. His mother, Queen Metinera, walked in during the ritual and thought Demeter meant to kill Demophon. She screamed, and Demeter pulled the boy from the fire when the ritual was complete. He was completely unharmed, and very much immortal.

Given that the Queen had reacted so badly to the first attempt, she instead taught Triptolemus the secret of agriculture, which he would teach to the rest of his kingdom so they could prosper. Triptolemus was regarded as Demeter's first priest and ambassador, and is usually seen in a winged chariot in the company of Demeter, Persephone, and Hecate.

Demeter was so revered that she was rarely insulted or driven to be wrathful or vengeful by the misconduct of mortals. However, there were exceptions.

Ascalabus was a son of Misme, who lived in Attica. During Demeter's search for Persephone, she came to Misme and was received kindly. She was exhausted and thirsty, and so was given something to drink. She was so thirsty she emptied the vessel in one draught, which made Ascalabus laugh at her. He then ordered a whole cask to be brought.

Demeter was indignant at the mocking comment, and sprinkled a few drops from her vessel on him, which turned him into a lizard.

A similar punishment happened to Ascalaphus, who was a spirit of the underworld. Demeter turned him into an owl – the myths may have been conflated because of the similarity in the words for spotted lizard (askalaxos) and the screech owl (askalaphos).

Erysichthon was another mortal man who inspired Demeter's wrath. He was king of Thessaly, and resided near a sacred grove to the goddess Demeter. Every tree grew in this grove, but in the center of it was a mighty oak tree. Erysichthon entered the grove and cut down the tree so he could build a banquet hall. When the tree fell, the dryad who lived in it died as

well, and the other dryads went to Demeter to demand punishment.

Demeter was happy to punish the arrogant king. She tasked Limos, the Greek goddess of hunger, to curse Erysichthon with insatiable hunger, in acknowledgement that her tree was going to be used for a banquet hall.

Never let it be said that the gods didn't have a sense of irony.

Erysichthon ate constantly, from the moment he woke to the moment he went to sleep, and was never satisfied. The more he ate, the more he seemed to go hungry. Demeter also sent the

ABOVE: Demeter, the goddess of agricultural abundance, stands at the left, holding a scepter. At the right is Persephone, her daughter and the wife of Hades, the god of the underworld. The boy is thought to be Triptolemos, who was sent by Demeter to teach men how to cultivate grain.

OPPOSITE: A marble statue of Demeter.

Oneiroi into his dreams, to ensure Erysichthon dreamed of banquets and food.

Driven by this insatiable hunger, Erysichthon's house soon ran out of food. He went on to eat all the horses and mules, but remained hungry. He then sold his own daughter, Mestra, to buy more food.

Mestra had been a lover of Poseidon, and did not want to be owned by anyone. She prayed to Poseidon, who gave her the ability to change shape. She was able to escape her buyer this way.

However, when Erysichthon realized Mestra had this gift, he knew he could sell her over and over again. He continued to buy food with it, until the money ran out, and Erysichthon eventually began to eat himself. He ate himself to his death.

Another example of Demeter's vengeful nature is when she sent her beloved Triptolemus to Lyncus, who was a king of Scythia (Sicily). Triptolemus brought gifts from Demeter and Lyncus, out of a desire to claim credit for the gifts, tried to kill him in his sleep. Just as he was about to put a knife into the heart of Triptolemus, Demeter turned him into a lynx.

The last significant example of Demeter's powers is with the sirens. The sirens were the companions and guardians of Persephone. After her abduction, Demeter gave them wings so they could fly over the world to find her. In a different version, she cursed them, for letting Persephone be taken.

ABOVE: Lyncus about to kill Triptolemus in his sleep. As he raises the knife, Demeter appears to save her beloved Triptolemus, and turns Lyncus into a lynx.

OPPOSITE: At the right, Persephone's pale body rises out of the underworld, where she is condemned to spend part of each year among the dead. She is supported by Hermes, the messenger of the gods, who wears a blue cloak and red-winged hat. On the left, Demeter greets her daughter with open arms. The reunion of Demeter and Persephone was associated with renewal and the changing of the seasons, evoked here by the warm blue sky and the sprig of almond blossom at Demeter's feet.

DIONYSUS

The youthful, beautiful, but effeminate god of wine. He is also called Bacchus both by Greeks and Romans. The noisy or riotous god.

ABOVE: Silenus with the baby Dionysus, a Roman marble copy from Greek original.

After Zeus managed to save Dionysus from his wife Hera, he changed him into the form of a kid and sent Hermes to give him to the nymphs who live on Mount Nysa.

Silienus, a pot-bellied, wine-drinking old Satyr, gifted with wisdom and prophecy, despite his uncouth appearance, was Dionysus' tutor and accompanied him on all his expeditions.

OPPOSITE: Bacchus painted by Caravaggio circa 1598.

Dionysus was the son of Zeus and Semele, who was a mortal woman having an affair with Zeus while Zeus was married to Hera.

Hera found out that Semele was pregnant, and disguised herself as a mortal, and befriended Semele. Semele confessed that she was pregnant with the child of Zeus, and Hera pretended not to believe her, convincing Semele to ask Zeus to reveal himself to her in his full glory.

Unfortunately for Semele, mortals were not able to look upon gods in their full glory, so when Zeus revealed himself to her, she burst into flames and died. Zeus saved Dionysus from her ashes and sewed him into the thigh of Zeus.

Once Dionysus was born, Zeus entrusted him to Hermes. In some stories, Persephone or Rhea took the baby and raised him. They then took the child to Ino and Athamas, where he was raised as a girl. Hera pursued Ino and Athamas, driving them to madness so that they would hurt the child. Zeus changed Dionysus into a ram and carried him to the nymphs of Mount Nysa.

The nymphs took the young Dionysus and raised him in a cave. Afterwards, they were rewarded by Zeus by being placed as Hyades among the stars. In addition to the nymphs, the Muses, Mystis, and Macris were said to have had a hand in his rearing, teaching him the mysteries and nursing him with honey. On

TOP: Dionysus scatters the pirates, who are changed into dolphins. North African mosaic, dated 2nd century AD.

ABOVE: Drinking vessel with a mask of Dionysos.

Mount Nysa, which is where the god got his name, Dionysus discovered and cultivated the vine, and invented wine during his youth.

When Dionysus grew up, Hera drove him mad, and he wandered all over the earth and through many countries. Two donkeys, which were afterwards sacred to Dionysus, carried him across a vast lake where he would have otherwise drowned. He wandered Egypt, Syria, and Asia, into India. He was not always well received, but his troupe of satyrs, Pans, and Bacchic women overcame most adversity. He established towns in India, and taught them the cultivation of the vine. The people there worshipped him as a god after he moved on.

While known as a merry god, Dionysus could also be severe. He passed through Thrace on his travels and was received badly by Lycurgus, king of the Edones. Dionysus leapt into the sea to take refuge with Thetis, the ocean Titaness, and rewarded her for her kindness with a golden urn which was made by Hephaestus.

Lycurgus had captured all of the women and satyr companions of Dionysus, though the women were quickly released. His country soon stopped bearing fruit and became barren, and Lycurgus went mad, killing his own son who he mistook for a vine tree. His madness was cured after this act, but the land remained barren. Dionysus said it would remain so, as punishment for arresting his friends and mistreating him, so the Edones took Lycurgus and put him in chains, and Dionysus had him torn to pieces by horses.

He proceeded on through Thrace without any further trouble, and arrived at Thebes, where he settled and ruled. He drove the women to quit their houses and join him in a feast. Pentheus, who ruled Thebes at the time, went to check on the riotous merrymaking, going to the mountains to try and bring the feverish women home. Agave, his mother, was in such a frenzy when he arrived that she mistook him for an animal, and tore him to pieces.

Dionysus then went on to Argos. The people there refused to acknowledge him as a god, so Dionysus drove the women there mad, to the point where they killed and devoured their own children. In one version of the story, Perseus encountered and killed many of the women that accompanied Dionysus, but the pair were reconciled, and the Argives began to worship the god and build him temples. It is in one of these temples that Ariadne, beloved of Dionysus, is buried.

The last feat of Dionysus was done during a voyage from Icaria to Naxos. He hired a ship, owned by Tyrrhenian pirates, who steered the ship past Naxos instead of landing there, and went to Asia intending to sell Dionysus on arrival. Dionysus learned of their plan and turned the oars and sail into serpents, and himself into a lion. He filled the ship with ivy and with sharp music made by flutes, which drove the sailors so mad they jumped into the sea. They then transformed into dolphins.

For those who welcomed Dionysus and were good to him, adopting his worship, he gave them wine and vines. Icarius of Athens was taught winemaking by Dionysus when he first arrived. He tried to share the gift, but his countrymen stoned him to death because they thought he had been possessed.

Erigone, daughter of Icarius, and his hound Maera, searched for him and found his body. His daughter hung herself, and the hound leapt into a well. Dionysus was enraged by their deaths and put them all in the stars, creating Bootes, Virgo, and Canis Major, before he turned his fury on the people.

He created a drought and drove the young maidens mad, to the point where they also hung themselves. The Athenians, desperate to put a stop to these inflictions, consulted an oracle, who told them to create a feast day. The Athenians did so, in the honor of dead heroes, and the god was appeased.

As Dionysus' adventures came to an end, his divinity was recognized and he was worshipped widely throughout the world. It was now time for him to ascend to Mount Olympus and become a fully-fledged god.

However, it was tradition that Dionysus needed to achieve one final great deed, which would prove his worthiness to be among the gods and live on Olympus. He needed to go into the Underworld and retrieve Semele, his mother. That was the only way he could demonstrate mastery over death itself, which was a frequent theme among gods and great heroes.

Dionysus went to the Underworld and successfully retrieved Semele, and Zeus granted him immortality and a seat on Olympus. It is widely believed that Hestia, the ever-gentle goddess of the hearth, gave up her seat to make room for Dionysus. Semele was renamed Thyone, and lived forever with Dionysus among the Olympian gods.

ABOVE: Ancient statue of Dionysus holding a cup of wine.

BELOW: Icarius was cordial towards Dionysus, who gave his shepherds wine. Here we see Icarius transporting wine, 3rd century mosaic from Paphos, Cyprus.

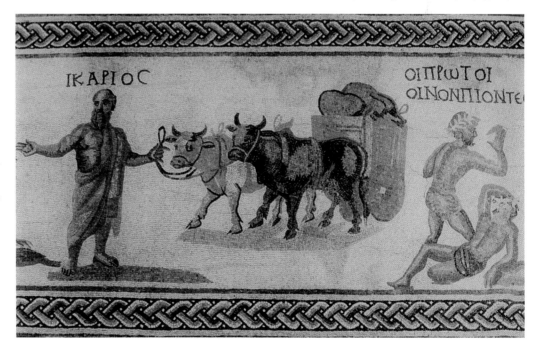

HEPHAESTUS

Hephaestus was originally created by Hera by herself, as revenge for Zeus 'giving birth' to Athena on his own.

However, he was so ugly and misshapen that she abandoned him on Lemnos, a Greek island where he grew up and honed his smithing skills under the care of the blacksmith Kidalionas. He later returned to Olympus, and became the smith of the gods, forging thunderbolts for Zeus, as well as jewelry, armor, and weapons for gods and mortals alike.

In one version, Hephaestus was not left at Lemnos but physically hurled from the heavens by Hera in a fit of disgust at his ugliness. He was severely injured on the way down, but survived. In this version, the sea nymphs Thetis and Eurynome found and took care of him as an infant. In another version, Hephaestus was cast out of Olympus for trying to save Hera, as Zeus was punishing her for her attempts to kill Heracles. Zeus was so enraged by the actions of the young Hephaestus that he flung the child from Olympus to Lemnos, and it was there that Hephaestus was cared for by a native tribe called the Sintians.

BELOW: The Doric temple of Hephaestus, Agora of Athens, Greece.

While Hephaestus had tried to help his mother in this instance, their relationship was far from peaceful. In the version where Hera was the one who threw him out of the heavens, Hephaestus got his revenge. He gifted Hera with a beautiful golden throne, crafted by his own hands. Hera was delighted by the gift and accepted it, but when she sat on her new throne, it trapped her in place.

The gods begged Hephaestus to release Hera, but he refused. That is until Dionysus, the god of wine, got him drunk, and Zeus himself advised that Hera should be released. Hephaestus wasn't a fool – he wanted something out of the exchange, and so he asked for Aphrodite's hand in marriage as payment for releasing Hera. Zeus felt he had no choice but to agree, and so the ugliest god on Olympus married the goddess of beauty herself.

Their marriage was turbulent, with both of them having children with seemingly everyone but each other. Aphrodite had lovers in gods and mortals alike. One such lover she had was Ares, and the two had a long affair until Helios the sun god spotted them mid-fling in the bed of Hephaestus. Helios was indignant and so sought out Hephaestus and told him everything, prompting Hephaestus to want revenge. He created an intricate net of golden threads, so thin it was barely visible, and set a trap on his bed. When Aphrodite and Ares were in bed together, the trap was sprung. Hephaestus invited all of the Olympians to see the couple and mock their humiliation.

When he wasn't getting revenge for past slights or having affairs of his own, Hephaestus was creating things. As thanks to Thetis for caring for him as a child, Hephaestus made a second set of armor for Achilles. Patroclus died in the first set, and Achilles wore this armor when he rejoined the battlefield in the Trojan War. He was wearing this armor when he killed Hector, Troy's greatest warrior.

ABOVE LEFT: Athena scorns the advances of Hephaestus.

ABOVE RIGHT: Marble statue of Hephaestus holding the tools he needs to forge armor, weapons and jewelry for gods as well as mortals.

Hephaestus created all of the palaces on Olympus for the gods and goddesses, the winged sandals and helmet worn by the messenger god Hermes, chariot of Helios, girdle of Aphrodite, arrows of Eros, sword of Perseus, breastplate of Diomedes, and arrows of Apollo, in addition to thunderbolts of Zeus and many other things.

Heracles used bronze clappers created by Hephaestus after Athena gave them to him. His sixth labor was to shoot down the Stymphalian Birds. Hephaestus also crafted a necklace for Harmonia, the daughter of Aphrodite and Ares, which was cursed to bring misfortune to whoever possessed it. This curse passed on to Harmonia's daughter, Semele, after Harmonia and Cadmus were turned into serpents.

Hephaestus, since he was lame and crippled,

created many automations that could help him work. He made handmaidens out of gold, who were able to understand, speak to, and assist him. He also made tripods that could walk, golden guard dogs, and created Talos, who was a giant bronze man tasked with protecting the island of Crete.

Pandora was one of the most lasting creations of Hephaestus, she was the first mortal woman. Zeus wanted her to be created after Prometheus had tricked Hephaestus and stolen fire for mankind from the god's forge. He obeyed and created Pandora from clay, and she was sent as a gift to Epimetheus, who was the less-discerning brother of Prometheus. Hephaestus also crafted the box full of misery that Pandora famously opened.

BELOW: Thetis receiving the weapons of Achilles from Hephaestus, by Anthony van Dyck, 1630-1632.

HEPHAESTUS God of Fire and the Forge, also the God of Blacksmithing. Revered by craftsmen, sculptors, metalworkers, and blacksmiths.

Symbol is a hammer, anvil, and pair of tongs.

Son of Hera, who conceived him on her own without Zeus. Often depicted as being crippled, lame, and very ugly.

Married to Aphrodite.

LEFT: Hephaestus and two assistants work on the arms for Achilles, the shield held up by Hephaestus and one of his assistants shows the mirror image of Thetis, sitting and watching the scene. Fresco from Pompeii, Italy.

Hermes was born in a cave on Mount Cyllene at dawn. On the day of his birth, he invented the lyre and could play a hymn celebrating his own birth. That same evening, he stole the cattle of Apollo, after which he innocently came back to his cradle and tucked himself in.

HERMES

In order to create the lyre, Hermes killed a tortoise and hollowed out its shell. He then stretched seven strings, in honor of the other Pleiades, made of sheep gut, and pulled them taut over the empty shell.

When he found out who had stolen his cattle, Apollo was very angry with Hermes and would have killed him. However, Hermes gave him the lyre as a gesture of appeasement. In exchange, Apollo forgave him and they became close friends, and Apollo gave Hermes his wand.

Hermes was universally loved by the gods, he was 'the darling' of the gods. Artemis taught him to hunt and Pan taught him how to play the pipes. Hermes was the one who guided Persephone back to Demeter, and Hermes was very close to his father, acting as wingman for Zeus and messenger when he was needed. Most famously, Hermes fought and beheaded the hundred-eyed giant Argus, who had been sent by Hera to watch over Io, one of the love interests of Zeus.

Since Hermes is the messenger, he is present in a great many myths. He escorted Pandora to Epimetheus, led Perseus to the Graeae, and guided Priam safely to the tent of Achilles. In addition, he showed Athena, Aphrodite, and Hera the way to Mount Ida where Paris was to judge which one of them was the fairest.

ABOVE: Terracotta statuett of Eros playing the lyre.

OPPOSITE: Battus is a shepherd who witnessed Hermes stealing Apollo's cattle. Because he broke his promise not to reveal this theft, Hermes turned him to stone.

ABOVE: Greek stamp from 1888 showing the head of Hermes.

ABOVE RIGHT: Marble statue of Hermes fastening the thongs of his winged sandal. His head is facing toward the heavens, as if he is hearing instructions from his father, Zeus.

BELOW: Marble statue of a hermaphrodite peacefully sleeping.

Hermes never married, and rarely took consorts and had children. He was in love with Aphrodite, but she didn't want anything to do with him. He became downcast, so Zeus had pity on him and sent an eagle to steal one of Aphrodite's sandals, carrying it far away eventually to be found by Hermes. When he brought the sandal back, she regarded him with favor and they had Hermaphrodites, Tyche, and Herse. At one time, Hermes and Apollo fell in love with Chione at the same time, and slept with her on the same day. Chione later gave birth to twins – Philammon took after Apollo, becoming a famous musician. Autolycus son of Hermes, became a trickster and a thief, taking after his father. Hermes was also the great-grandfather of Odysseus, who may have inherited his cleverness and penchant for trickery from his divine bloodline.

Hermes was a very clever god, and because he was so fiercely loyal to his father Zeus, he knew that he needed to have Hera as an ally as well. Hera was quick to anger over the many affairs of Zeus and Hermes became caught in the crossfire.

To resolve this, he disguised himself as Ares, Hera's son, and climbed up into her lap. She didn't see through his deception, and began to breastfeed him, which made Hermes into her honorary child. Being treated as a foster child, Hera was now obliged to treat Hermes as her son, which brought an end to conflict between the two.

When Zeus revealed himself to Semele, she burst into flames while pregnant with Dionysus. Zeus saved the baby and gave him to Hermes ordering Hermes to hide Dionysus from Hera's wrath. Hermes swiftly absconded with the baby and took him to a remote mountain, where he was raised by nymphs and eventually joined the rest of the gods on Olympus.

HERMES Son of Zeus and Maia, the oldest of the seven Pleiades.

Winged messenger and herald of the gods.

A trickster, god of roads, flocks, commerce, and thieves.

Originally portrayed as a mature bearded man, more recent and popular depictions of Hermes show him as an athletically built youth, wearing a broad-brimmed hat, winged sandals, a purse, and a wand, which is a short-winged staff circled by two serpents.

Credited with the invention of speech, and associated with interpretation.

Also known as 'the conductor', 'the leader of souls', the patron of travelers and thieves, 'shepherd of men', and 'Argus-slayer'.

LEFT: Marble statue of Hermes carrying Dionysus. Hermes needed to hide him from the wrath of Hera, and so took him to a remote mountain where he was raised by nymphs.

HESTIA

VESTAE   SACRVM
C. PVPIVS FIRMINVS ET
  MVDASENA   TROPHIME

GODDESS OF THE HEARTH.

TOP RIGHT: Sitting on her throne, Hestia carries a staff in her left hand.

ABOVE: Trade cards from the "Goddesses of the Greeks and Romans" in a set of 50 cards in 1889 by W.S. Kimball & Co.

Hestia is the Greek goddess of the hearth, and one of the original Olympians, the first-born child of Cronus and Rhea. Hestia was a pure and peaceful goddess, who stayed at home and tended the fireplace.

Because of her relative reclusivity, preferring to stay at home and keep the hearth, she is not included in many myths. Later, she would be replaced in the pantheon with Dionysus, after surrendering her place on Olympus so that he could join the rest of the gods.

Since making and preserving fire was an essential part of life for the Ancient Greeks, Hestia's role as keeper of the hearth was an important one, and central to Ancient Greeks' social and religious life. Hestia was not only

goddess of the hearth, but the embodiment of it.

She is usually portrayed as a modest, middle-aged woman, wearing a veil and standing by a large fire. She either carries a staff or flowers in her hands. Her other names included 'Beloved', 'Eternal', and 'She of the public hearth'.

Fire was known to the Ancient Greeks as a pure and purifying element, and so Hestia was worshipped as a virgin goddess. She remained a virgin, according to myth, to preserve the peace on Olympus, because both Apollo and Poseidon

wanted to marry her and she feared that choosing one of them would result in aggression between them. She swore to eternal virginity by placing her hand on the head of Zeus, and as a reward, Zeus granted her the central place in the house – the fireplace – and the first and richest portion of human divine offerings.

For the most part, Hestia's chastity was secure. One time, at a feast, the god of fertility, Priapus, had a little too much wine and tried to rape Hestia while she slept.

Fortunately, a donkey was nearby and began to bray, waking both Hestia and the rest of the guests, who chased Priapus away. Since that night, donkeys were given rest and garlands on Hestia's feast day.

Aside from these myths, Hestia does not appear, nor does she participate in processions through the heavens, as she is always at home tending to the fire. Later stories passed down say that the sound of crackling fire is Hestia's gentle laughter.

TOP RIGHT: Priapus, who tried to rape Hestia, laden down with fresh food to eat.

BELOW: The Temple of Hestia, in Rome, Italy. This photo was taken around 1850s.

3

SPIRITS, MONSTERS, AND OTHER GODS

SPIRITS, MONSTERS, AND OTHER GODS

Typhon and Echidna were the father and mother of monsters, humanoid hybrids, and creatures with incredible physiognomy. These creatures were often featured as villains in the myths, either as symbols to warn of inexplicable horror, or to the dangers of offending the gods.

The winged horse Pegasus was known to be friendly and helpful, however, there were others, particularly the centaurs, who were known to be noisy and aggressive. The centaur Chiron was an exception and was known for his wisdom and knowledge of medicine. There was also the Sphinx with the body of a lion and head of a woman. The Harpies were birds with the heads and upper bodies of women. The Cyclopes were one-eyed giants who forged the thunderbolt for Zeus.

Circe was the sorceress who was able to change humans into animals with the use of drugs and incantations. The Fates were a trio of goddesses often to be shown spinning or weaving. Certain creatures appeared to be humanoid, but possessed otherworldly power, which they used to help or hinder the various gods and heroes.

Greeks had a myth for every eventuality, often they concerned monsters which were slain by heroes in epic battles. Automatons were metal men created by Hephaestus who was blacksmith to the gods. Manticores had the head of a man, the body of a lion and the tail of a scorpion: and was the embodiment of evil. Almost as fearsome was the fire-breathing chimera, with the body of a lion, the head of a goat protruding from its back and a snakes-head tail. Unicorns on the other hand represented purity, gentleness, magic and innocence. Many of these creatures have become almost as well known as the gods, goddesses and heroes who share their stories.

A marble statue of Heracles and the centaur Nessus. By the scultpor Giambologna 1598, in the Piazza Signoria, Florence, Italy.

During the Titanomachy, Atlas fought on the side of the Titans, and even became the leader of the rebellion against Zeus. However, this meant that after the Titans lost, he received the heaviest punishment by Zeus. Atlas was condemned to hold up the Heavens for eternity, standing near the garden of his daughters, the Hesperides.

ATLAS

ATLAS One of the original Titans, the son of Iapetus and Clymene, brother to Prometheus, Menoetius, and Epimetheus.
Father to the goddess-nymph Calypso, and the Pleiades by Pleione. Aethra bore him the Hyades and Hyas, only son of Atlas. Atlas also married Hesperis and fathered the Hesperides.
His name can be translated to 'very enduring'.
Usually portrayed as a large, very muscled bearded man, always slightly bent and appearing to be in great pain under the weight of holding up the sky.

Depending on the legend, Atlas either has the sky directly braced on his shoulders, or he is responsible for holding the two pillars that separate the earth and the sky, making sure that they don't collapse and cause the sky to fall.

As Atlas was unable to move, the only two myths in which he is involved are those of Heracles, and Perseus. Heracles journeyed to the Hesperidean garden to retrieve a few of the golden apples that grew there. Eurystheus was the hero chosen by Hera to give the twelve labors to Heracles. Heracles bargained with Atlas to retrieve apples from the garden of his daughter as he could do so without alerting the dragon which guarded them. In return Heracles would bear the burden of the sky for a short time.

Atlas retrieved the apples, but he planned to deliver them to Eurystheus himself and leave Heracles in his place, thus freeing himself from his torment. However, when he told Heracles this plan, Heracles tricked Atlas by asking him to take the weight of the sky back just for a moment, so that Heracles could adjust his position. When Atlas took the sky back, Heracles simply took the golden apples and left Atlas to his fate.

The second – and last – hero to visit Atlas was Perseus. Perseus passed by Atlas after killing Medusa and asked the Titan for hospitality. Atlas was afraid of being tricked and humiliated again, so he refused. In retribution, Perseus showed Atlas the severed head of Medusa, which turned him into stone.

ABOVE: Heracles and Atlas, painted on beech wood by Lucas Cranach the Elder (1472–1553), after 1537

OPPOSITE: Atlas Supporting the Globe, ca. 1780. Terracotta, painted to resemble bronze.

CIRCE

Circe's most famous encounter was with Odysseus, when he and his men landed on her island. Their journey had been long and arduous, and Odysseus and his men sought shelter. They didn't know where they were, and the island was shrouded in mystery.

A group of Odysseus' men disappeared when Circe lured them into her mansion. She gave them food and they were transformed into swine by her magic. Odysseus would also have succumbed but Hermes had given him a potion to resist the magic of Circe, so he was spared.

Circe and Odysseus became lovers, and during this time Circe transformed his men back into their original forms. They lived in paradise on the island for a year. Circe is said to have borne three sons from Odysseus: Agrius, Latinus, and Telegonus.

When it was time for Odysseus to leave, Circe helped him to return home. She told Odysseus how to enter the Underworld so that he could speak to Tiresias. Circe then told Odysseus how to travel safely between Scylla and Charybdis.

Circe is credited with the creation of Scylla, and transformation is a common theme in her tales. Circe was in love with Glaucus, a minor sea deity, but Glaucus was in love with a beautiful maiden named Scylla. Some stories say that Circe poisoned the bathwater of Scylla, in others Circe gave Glaucus a love potion. However, the potion of Glaucus transformed Scylla into a hideous many-headed monster, who was famous for destroying ships on the cliffs opposite the massive whirlpool, Charybdis.

Circe also fell in love with Picus, one of the sons of Cronus. She tried to seduce him, but Picus rejected her, as he was in love with Caenns, who was a daughter of the Roman god Janus. When Picus rejected the advances of Circe, she became enraged, and cursed Picus with a spell that transformed him into a woodpecker.

When the friends of Picus came looking for him, they were unaware of the curse and his transformation, Circe turned them into animals as well, and these became the foundation for many of the animals who lived on Mount Circaeum in the following years.

BELOW: Fresco of the followers of Odysseus being turned back to human form by Circe. Painted by Giovanni Battista Trotti, 1610.

CIRCE Daughter of the Greek sun god Helios and the Oceanid Perse (Perseis), sister of Pasiphae, Perses, and Aeetes, and aunt to Medea.

Regarded as one of the most powerful sorceresses of Greek mythology.

Known to call upon the aid of 'dark' deities such as Chaos, Nyx, and Hecate.

Lived on the island of Aeaea, where she had been brought by her father Helios, in his golden chariot. She lived in a mansion within a forest clearing and was attended by nymphs, and kept a large collection of 'domesticated' wild beasts as companions.

RIGHT: Circe Offering the Cup to Odysseus. John William Waterhouse, 1891.

BELOW: Circe turns Odysseus' companions into animals. Woodcut, hand colored.

CHARON

Charon, the eternal ferryman for the dead, was one of many residents in the Greek Underworld.

There were five major rivers in the Underworld, the two most famous being the River Acheron, and the River Styx. Originally, Charon was said to be the ferryman of the River Acheron but in later mythology the River Styx became more dominant and so Charon is known as the ferryman of the River Styx.

When a person died, the soul was escorted down to the banks of the River, where Charon would be waiting with his boat – provided, of course, that the deceased were in possession of a coin to pay for the journey.

Charon transported souls across the River in exchange for either an obolos, or a Persian denace. These coins were ideally placed in the mouth of the corpse during a funeral, and so provided proof that the deceased had been given proper funeral rites. While the coins themselves were not particularly valuable, it was essential that they were provided to the dead. Charon would not ferry souls across the River without a coin, and if they could not cross, they were cursed to wander the banks of the River for 100 years, and their spirits would haunt those on Earth who had denied them proper funeral rites during this time.

If the deceased were in possession of a coin, then Charon would safely ferry them across the

River and into the domain of Hades. They would then go on to be judged on how they would spend eternity in the Underworld.

Charon was not supposed to allow the living into the Underworld, but there are a few notable exceptions: Psyche, whom he allowed to pass in her search for Eros, and who paid Charon to allow her to pass; Theseus, when he sought to abduct Persephone from the Underworld, and who may have paid Charon as well, or used his cunning to dupe the ferryman; Orpheus, who charmed Charon with a melody; Aeneas, who won passage to the Underworld in exchange for the magical Golden Bough; and Heracles (Hercules), who was said to have bested Charon in a physical contest and wrestled him into submission, or intimidated the ferryman by frowning at him.

In later myths, Charon is said to have been punished for each of these instances where he allowed a living person to enter the Underworld. Hades would punish Charon each time by putting him in chains for one year. In these legends there is no information as to whether the deceased simply had to wait, or whether Charon had a replacement who ferried people across in his absence.

Charon ferrying the sinners on his boat across to the underworld.

ERIS

Eris was not only the goddess of discord and hostility, but she represented negative emotions, strife, and argumentative chaos. She deliberately fostered discord between people, gods and mortals alike, and delighted in the harm these arguments caused.

ERIS Goddess of strife and discord, who essentially started or was at the heart of every disagreement and argument in Ancient Greece.

Sometimes said to be the daughter of Zeus and Hera, but most often depicted as the daughter of Erebus (Darkness) and Nyx (Night).

Eris was depicted, when first arriving at a place, as a very small woman, dwarfed even by children and animals. However, the longer she stayed in one place, the larger she grew, symbolizing how discord can fester and feed on itself until it's large enough to reach the heavens.

Eris enjoyed the unhappiness of others and sought to create it wherever she went. She was credited with arguments among friends, or engendering feelings of infidelity and distrust among married couples. The vicious fights and centuries of distrust between Zeus and Hera, were notorious among mortals and gods alike, and gave rise to the desire of their daughter to cause discord.

Eris fostered jealousy, and resentment as well as distrust. Typically she was seen as an impartial goddess; she never took sides in an argument, simply liked to watch them happen. She was harsh and mean-spirited and would start fights whenever she was able to.

In any argument, large or small, she was said to be the first to instigate it and the last to leave. Even after the fighting was done, strife and resentment often stayed behind.

Most of all, though, Eris embodied the strife of war. She was often seen as a companion of Ares, the god of chaotic war filled with blood lust and brutality. Strife and discord thrived on a battlefield, and Eris shared the delight of Ares in the horrors of battle.

Eris famously, was not forbidden by Zeus from getting involved in the Trojan War. Since Eris didn't pick sides, she was the only deity present during the scenes of battles. She didn't need to choose a side to delight in the hatred and misery that affected both sides of in a war.

There are many depictions of war scenes where a woman stands in the middle of it all. This is often assumed to be Eris, however there is another goddess, who is also the companion of Ares and shares his love of war, called Enyo. In the writings of Homer, he uses these names interchangeably and doesn't distinguish between the two goddesses, so they could simply be the same person under different names.

They were both ideal companions for Ares, who loved the violence and destruction of war. Both goddesses were noted for their destructive natures and quarrelsome personalities. Enyo, the 'sacker of cities', and Eris, of strife and discord, were both unwelcome by all men.

Eris is given credit for motivation in one particular place: the Greek writer Hesiod states that Eris was responsible for toil in the

field, and for competition among neighbors, which would eventually improve the lives of the whole community. This was a form of strife that, according to Hesiod, was beneficial. The outward Eris that was focused on battle was often confused with Enyo, whereas the inward Eris that caused men to fight against their own bad habits and inspired them to work hard, was thought to be a different type of goddess.

Eris had many children, giving birth to several negative beings in myth. Most of these children were simply ways to personify feelings and troubles that were caused by strife. There was Ponos, who represented backbreaking labor that was necessary to survive poverty. Lethe, the goddess of forgetfulness, and Limos, who personified extreme hunger such as the famines that happened after wars.

There were the Algae – Lupa, Ania, and Achos – who were three sisters that represented both mental and physical pain. The Hysminai were spirits of hand-to-hand combat of brawls and fistfights. The Machae represented the loud clash of noise on a battlefield and the confusing sound of war, and the Androctasiae represented

killings within the realm of warfare. The Phonoi personified murder, killing, and slaughter that were not in the context of war,

There was also Horcus, who was god of oaths, Ate, a daimon of impulsiveness and recklessness, Dysnomia, who engendered lawlessness and lack of civil order, and the altercations of the Amphilogiae. The Pseudologoi spread lies and the Neikea arguments and feuds. These were the most malevolent children of Eris, who embodied feuds and lasting grievances.

ABOVE: The wedding of Thetis and Peleus. Eris wasn't invited, enraged, she stole a golden apple from the Hesperides and threw it into the middle of Athena, Hera and Aphrodite to fight over.

BELOW: Detail from a frieze on an ancient Greek temple showing the Trojan war, Delphi, Greece.

OPPOSITE: Eris shown here on the side of a terracotta pot.

Antique columns in Troy, off the coast of the Aegaen Sea, Turkey.

The most famous story involving Eris is, of course, that of the golden apple. When Thetis and Peleus were to be married, everyone was invited except for Eris.

She didn't take well to the rejection, and stole a golden apple from the Hesperides. She left a note with it saying that it belonged to the 'fairest', and threw it into the middle of Athena, Hera, and Aphrodite. Of course the three immediately began to fight over the apple, and it fell to Paris, the Trojan prince to decide. Zeus

was unwilling to risk losing favor with any of the three goddesses.

Hera was his wife, Athena was his daughter, and Aphrodite was his half-sister. Whichever choice he made would be an insult to the others that would not only continue their conflict, but bring the anger of two powerful goddesses into his personal life.

The three goddesses appeared before Paris for his judgement. Hera offered Paris power and land, Athena offered victory in battle and

wisdom, and Aphrodite who offered the love of the most beautiful woman in the world was the winner. Unfortunately, at the time, the most beautiful woman in the world was Helen, who was already married to the Spartan king. Aphrodite kept her word and caused Helen to fall in love with Paris, and the couple eloped to Troy.

This 'abduction', or runaway wife according to whether you believe Helen went willingly or not, initiated the Trojan War. Sparta called upon their allies in Greece and sailed to Troy to lay siege to the city.

The war lasted for ten years, and many great heroes, mortals, and demigods were lost in the fighting. The war was so all-consuming that it split much of Olympus in half, with gods and goddesses aiding their favored heroes on either side.

True to her nature, Eris did not pick a side. She remained in the center of the battlefield, watching it all with delight.

Eros was the youngest of the gods and often seen as a companion of Aphrodite. He was a mischievous character, often firing his arrows of passionate love into the hearts of mortals and gods alike. He also has a connection with homosexual love due to a relationship with Ares.

EROS

ABOVE: A Roman statue of Pothos, a follower of Eros.

ABOVE RIGHT: Eros shoots his arrow of love. This statue is at Piccadilly Circus, London, England.

There are a few different accounts for his origins. Some wrote that Eros was a primordial being, a child of Chaos, and blessed the union between Uranus and Gaia. He was seen as a facilitator between the unions of other primordial deities. Eros was a positive and negative character in myths, since his unions could be miserable as often as they were prosperous and joyful.

In later versions of his myth, Eros was said to be the son of Aphrodite, with conflicting beliefs as to who his father was. Some thought it could be Hermes, some Zeus, but in most versions of his myth he is the son of Aphrodite and Ares is his father.

Eros was the god of love – specifically, the god of passionate or carnal love. The Greeks noted that there were many types of love. Eros with his arrows, was able to make anyone fall in love instantly, however the love was not considered lasting or 'deep', and never stronger than a physical attraction. His specific kind of love was considered sexual, which explains why Eros was also associated with fertility.

Anteros, brother of Eros, was considered a god of love, but the quieter kind. Love that had been requited, and he was associated with the concept of mutual love. Anteros was seen as a vengeful god in contrast to his more playful brother, who took action against those who rejected the love of others.

Anteros and Eros are seen as opposites and are shown to be on opposite scales of each other. However, their physical appearances are quite similar and statues of Anteros are often confused with those of Eros.

Eros had several followers or minor deities he was associated with: Pothos and Himeros were commonly seen by his side, and represented longing and desire. The Erotes were a few winged gods that were associated with love and desire. Their numbers varied and they have no distinct mythology.

The story of Eros and Psyche is one of the most well-known love stories in all of Greek mythology. Psyche was the youngest of three daughters of a king, and possessed a beauty that had never been seen before. She was so beautiful that people began to forget about Aphrodite, thus leading to her temples being abandoned. Aphrodite began to fade from existence due to lack of followers.

Aphrodite commanded Eros to use his power to aid her. She wanted Psyche to fall in love with the most vile, despicable man on the planet. Eros was meant to do this with one of his arrows, however, when he laid eyes on her, he instantly fell in love as well.

Eros was then faced with a choice: to do as he had been bidden by his mother, or to submit to his love and risk his mother's anger. Eventually, he decided that he would ignore Aphrodite's request and spare Psyche a terrible match.

Psyche was incredibly lonely, cursed by her beauty. She was unable to make a meaningful connection since everyone who fell in love with her simply wanted to worship her, and no man dared approach her. Her sisters were both married, and the king eventually was so desperate to help his daughter that he sought the advice of the Oracle of Delphi. He asked Apollo what he could do to find Psyche a husband.

Apollo told the king to take Psyche to the summit of a mountain, wearing a black dress. Once alone a terrifying winged serpent would take her for its wife. This news devastated her family, but Psyche dutifully donned her dress and climbed the mountain. She waited on top of the mountain for hours in the cold, until she suddenly felt a wind, which carried her into the air, eased her pain, and sent her to sleep.

When she woke, she was in a meadow of flowers in front of a magical castle which belonged to a god. She approached the castle, and heard a voice telling her not to be afraid, that she was free to enter and bathe before they celebrated her arrival.

Psyche did so and then waited for her husband. His voice was instantly soothing to her and she was overwhelmed with joy that she had married such a man. She spent most of the day in the castle waiting for him to join her in the evening, but was always happy in his presence.

Psyche was, however, unable to see her husband, and that saddened her. She asked him to see her family, and though he initially refused, when he saw how sad that answer made her, he allowed it. He warned her, however, that she must not allow her sisters to influence her mental state, otherwise their relationship would be destroyed and full of suffering.

Psyche's sisters arrived the following day. They were overwhelmed with happiness for Psyche's fortune and full of questions about her life in the castle and her husband. Psyche told them that he was a young hunter despite all the riches surrounding her. The sisters felt that she was lying and were consumed by jealousy, knowing that their happiness was no match for Psyche's, and therefore conspired to hurt her.

ABOVE: Brothers Eros and Anteros play while Psyche watches them.

BELOW: A young girl defends herself against the arrow of Eros. Painting by William Adolphe Bouguereau, circa 1880.

They taunted her saying that this mysterious husband must really be the evil snake, and that is why he was never seen, and that they pitied her.

Despite Psyche doing her best not to allow herself to be swayed by her sisters' words, she felt the first seeds of doubt being planted. She didn't know why her husband never visited her in the day and never showed his physical form. She determined that when he was asleep, she would light a candle and be able to see him. If he was a snake, she would kill him – if he wasn't, she would douse her flame and sleep happy.

Later that night, Psyche carried out her plan. She lit her candle and approached him, only to reveal the most handsome man she had ever seen. Psyche was ashamed by her lack of trust, and when she went to douse her flame, hot wax fell on her husband and woke him.

Eros had originally believed that true love between a god and a mortal was not possible, and that was why he hid his form from Psyche. He was heartbroken that she did not trust him, and left their bedroom, saying, "Love cannot live without trust."

Psyche realized that her husband was Eros, the god of love, and despaired over the fact that she hadn't been able to trust him. She wept for days before deciding that she would prove her love to Eros. She visited Aphrodite's temple and prayed to the goddess, asking her to persuade Eros to take her back.

Aphrodite, however, was still jealous and wanted revenge for Psyche ruining her worshippers and causing her temples to fade away. She told Psyche that she would have to prove herself with a series of tasks, and only then would Aphrodite help her.

First, Psyche was shown thousands of different seeds and told to separate them. Aphrodite wanted the hard work and labor to

ABOVE: Aphrodite and Eros on either side of a terracotta incense burner.

LEFT: Marble statue of Eros embracing Psyche. Uffizi Gallery, Florence, Italy.

OPPOSITE: Psyche being abducted by Eros. Painted by William Adolphe Bouguereau, 1895.

affect Psyche's beauty. Psyche wept at the task, for there were so many, it would take forever to sort, and she didn't know how to sort them. Her cries alerted a nearby colony of ants, who took pity on her and helped her sort the seeds.

The second task was for Psyche to make a fleece out of the golden sheep that lay across the river. When Psyche swam across, a spirit appeared to her to warn her how dangerous the sheep were. To avoid being killed by the sheep, Psyche should instead collect the fleece from the nearby bushes where the sheep had shed their wool. Psyche heeded the spirit's advice and managed to complete the task successfully.

Aphrodite then bade Psyche climb a waterfall that led to the River Styx, and fill a bottle she had been given. The rocks were far too slippery for Psyche to climb and again the task seemed impossible. To her surprise, an eagle flew over the river, took the bottle from her, and filled it with the water from the River Styx.

Aphrodite was beginning to grow angry that Psyche was receiving so much help and completing these tasks. The final task must

be completed by Psyche alone, she said, to prove that Psyche was truly determined to win Eros back.

For Psyche's last task, she was given a box to take to the Underworld, and she would have to ask Persephone to place some of her beauty inside of it. Psyche took the perilous journey through the Underworld and asked Persephone to drop some of her beauty in the box. Persephone was more than happy to assist Psyche, and did so. When Psyche returned to earth, she was overcome with curiosity and wanted to open the box. If it contained pure beauty, Psyche wanted to open it and become even more beautiful for her husband. However, when she opened the box, there was no beauty inside, only sleep. Aphrodite had tricked her, causing Psyche to fall into a deep slumber.

At this point, the rest of the gods had been watching and decided enough was enough. Hermes delivered a messaged to Eros, informing him of the trials and misfortunes Psyche had undergone to win his love back. Overcome by what he heard, Eros began to forgive his wife's betrayal and left his room in search of Psyche. He found her and was able to wake her from her sleep.

Overjoyed at seeing her husband again, they embraced happily and were reconciled. The men on earth had forgotten Psyche at this point, and once again began to worship Aphrodite as the true goddess of beauty, which prompted Aphrodite to move past her vengeance and leave the couple alone.

EROS The god of passionate love.

In some myths he is the son of Erebus (Darkness) and Nyx (Night), while in others he is the son of Ares.

The companion of Aphrodite.

Often depicted in conjunction with the Roman god Cupid, though his myths and roles are not quite the same. He was depicted as a plump, overweight child carrying a bow, and often said to be extremely beautiful.

HYPNOS

Hera twice used the gifts of Hypnos for inducing sleep in Zeus, the first time it was to settle feuds between the King and Queen of gods. Hera asked Hypnos to put Zeus to sleep, so that Zeus would be unable to aid his son.

ABOVE: The marble head of Hypnos

Hera called up a storm of strong winds to disrupt Heracles from sailing home after the sacking of Troy. When Zeus awoke and discovered what Hera had done, he became enraged and tried to punish Hypnos. The problem was, that Nyx was the mother of Hypnos, and Zeus was terrified of her. Hypnos hid with his mother when he knew Zeus was in pursuit. He managed to avoid punishment for his involvement because Zeus wanted to avoid Nyx.

The second time Hera asked for special intervention from Hypnos, it was because Hera wanted to help the Danaans to win the Trojan war. She came up with a plan to seduce Zeus. She fooled Aphrodite, the goddess of love, into giving her aromatic oils and a charm. Once she had everything prepared, Zeus had taken Hera in his arms, and Hypnos put Zeus to sleep once more.

Hypnos wasn't eager to help a second time, remembering how angry Zeus had been. The key to getting Hypnos to go along with Hera's plan was Pasithea. Hypnos was enamored of her, and agreed to help Hera after he had been promised that he could marry Pasithea.

Once Zeus was asleep, Hypnos went to the Achaean ships, and told Poseidon, the god of the Sea, that Zeus was asleep and would not interfere during the coming battle. This gave Poseidon plenty of time to assist the Danaans and turn the tide of the war towards Hera's desired outcome. This time, Zeus was unaware that Hypnos had been involved.

HYPNOS Son of Nyx (Night) and Erebus (Darkness), two of the primordial gods that predated Zeus. Brother of Thanatos, the god of death.

Personified and represented as sleep, characterized as a calm and gentle god.

Said to live in the Underworld, in a cave where one of the Underworld Rivers, the River Lethe, flowed. In his cave was a bed of ebony, and this was surrounded by poppies and other sleep-inducing plants. No light penetrated the cave, allowing Hypnos to sleep peacefully.

In the Iliad, the home of Hypnos was the island of Lemnos in the Aegean Sea. His island was described as 'dream-like'.

Hypnos married Pasithea, one of the Greek Charities or Graces, who was the personification of relaxation. Together they conceived the Oneiroi, the bringers of dreams.

LEFT: La Nuit (The Night), painted by William Adolphe Bouguereau, 1883.

The most notable myth of Nemesis is her involvement with Narcissus and Echo.

NEMESIS

NEMESIS Daughter of Nyx (Night) and Erebus (Darkness), according to Hesiod. In some myths she was the daughter of the titan Oceanus.

Goddess of divine retribution and revenge. She especially targeted mortals guilty of hubris or arrogance. She was often described as being utterly without remorse.

ABOVE RIGHT: Marble bust of Nemesis, Athens, Greece.

RIGHT: Painting by Pierre Paul Prud'hon called Justice and Divine Vengeance pursuing crime, 1808. Justice is on the left and Divine Vengeance (Nemesis), is on the right, they are pursuing the murderer. At the bottom of the painting is the dead man the criminal has just killed.

Narcissus was renowned as one of the most beautiful men in the world, but he was so arrogant and conceited that he believed himself to be superior to everyone else and showed disdain for anyone who tried to express their love for him. Because he was so beautiful, there were a lot of spurned lovers.

Echo was a nymph, who belonged to a large group of water and wood nymphs that were regularly visited by Zeus. He would visit them, and dance and play, much to their delight. Hera, wife of Zeus and a goddess renowned for her jealousy and temper, would often come searching for Zeus to catch him being unfaithful.

On one such occasion, Echo approached Hera and distracted her with lively chatter, leading her in circles around the forest while Zeus escaped detection with the other nymphs. When Hera realized she was being tricked, she flew into a rage and cursed Echo, so that she would only be able to repeat the last few words of whatever someone else said to her. She would literally become an 'echo'.

One day, Echo was wandering the woods, despondent since she had been abandoned by her friends after being cursed, when she spied a beautiful golden-haired man. It was Narcissus, alone in the woods while he was hunting. She fell in love with him immediately and followed him. When he realized someone was near, he called out to them, but of course Echo could only repeat his words back to him:

"Who is here?"

"Here!"

"Come to me!"

"To me, to me!"

Narcissus tried to find the source of the voice, but Echo evaded detection. She couldn't speak properly, and feared him rejecting her. When Narcissus finally said, "Let us meet!", she echoed him and revealed herself, only for him to immediately shove her away and claim that he would rather die than be with her. She wasn't good enough for someone as beautiful as him.

Nemesis loved to humble and humiliate arrogant mortals, but she also took pity on Echo, and wanted to punish Narcissus. She led Narcissus to a motionless pool with a perfect reflection in the middle of the forest. When Narcissus stopped for a drink, he immediately became transfixed by the sight of his own reflection in the water. However, he could not kiss or touch his reflection, and became more and more distraught with passing time. He was unable to tear his gaze away from the pool, so he didn't eat or sleep and ended up wasting away staring at his own reflection. He left a single beautiful bloom – the narcissus flower – in his place.

After Narcissus had rejected Echo, she wandered the mountains and found a lonely cave in which to live. She remained there and, upon learning of the death of Narcissus, became inconsolable. She did not eat or sleep, and continued to waste away until all that remained was her voice.

ABOVE: Engraving by Albrecht Dürer of Nemesis, circa 1502

BELOW: Narcissus stares at his own reflection, in love with himself. By Caravaggio, circa 1600.

PAN

Pan was born with goat legs, and goat horns on his head. His appearance delighted the gods, and he was a noisy, precocious, merry child.

ABOVE RIGHT: Bronze statue of Pan.

ABOVE: Seated Pan, who holds a pipe in his left hand and rests his right hand behind his torso. By Odoardo Fialetti, circa 1600-1630

However, mortals and nymphs were less enthused with his appearance and would often be startled or run away from him and his antics.

It is considered that Pan was given his name because he delighted all of the immortals, as 'Pan' translates to 'all'. Pan lived in Arcadia, in the wild mountains and rustic central region of Peloponnese. He would wander the forest, playing his pipes, chasing nymphs, and sleeping when tired.

Pan loved his naps, so much that it was considered very dangerous to try to awaken him. He was known to let out the worst blood-curdling wail if he was woken up, which, like the scream of a banshee, was said to inspire fear and anxiety in all who heard it. This explains the word panic as being the second meaning of his name.

Variously named: the pan pipes and pan flute were formed from reeds. Syrinx in escaping from Pan was helped by the river gods to turn herself into reeds. When Pan embraced them they made music which so delighted him, he turned them into a musical instrument.

Pan was so proficient at playing these pipes that he challenged Apollo to a contest. He lost the contest to the god of music, as Midas was the only one who said Pan had won. This prompted Apollo to give Midas his famous donkey ears.

Syrinx wasn't the only nymph Pan pursued. He was so odd-looking to mortals that they didn't return his love. Pitys was another nymph who turned into a plant rather than submit to Pan, on this occasion, it was a pine tree. Echo was too infatuated with Narcissus to notice Pan.

Pan did manage to trick and conquer Selene, the goddess of the moon. He wrapped himself in sheepskin and lured her into the woods while she was riding her silver chariot.

Pan didn't get involved in wars on a regular basis, preferring instead his lifestyle of playing

music, chasing nymphs, and taking naps. He did however, join Hermes in the quest to save Zeus during one of his many battles against the great Typhon, the father of all monsters. During one battle, the thunderbolts of Zeus were no match for Typhon, who dragged Zeus into a cave and removed his tendons to prevent escape. Hermes and Pan went to the cave and replaced his tendons, pushing his muscles back into place so that Zeus could heal.

In the first years of the Christian era, an Egyptian sailor named Thamus heard 'the great god Pan is dead' coming from the sky. If this account is accurate, it means that Pan is one of the very few gods of Ancient Greece that actually dies.

PAN Son of Hermes and a Dryad nymph.

Half man, half goat, the god of wild groves, shepherds, and flocks.

Often pictured with his iconic pan flute, which he created after the nymph Syrinx transformed herself into marsh reeds to escape his advances. Pan cut the reeds and made the pipe flute out of them, and was rarely seen without the instrument thereafter.

LEFT: Pan and Syrinx, by Jacob Jordaens, circa 1620.

BELOW: Statue of Pan playing his reed pipes.

PERSEPHONE

In classical Greek art, Persephone is always depicted as a venerable queen.

PERSEPHONE Daughter of Demeter and Zeus, wife of Hades and Queen of the Underworld.

Other names: Kore, Persephoneia, Persephassa, Persephatta, Pherepapha, Periphona, Phersephassa. Roman name: Proserpina

A dual deity, both of the dead and a goddess of fertility.

Often depicted holding a sheaf of wheat, or a cornucopia, or alongside Demeter with a four-pronged torch.

She is shown either carrying symbols of fertility and harvest, such as the cornucopia or 'horn of plenty', or her torch whenever she was portrayed with her mother, Demeter, who was the goddess of the seasons and harvest. Persephone could often be referred to as 'the maiden' or 'the mistress', and the two of them together as 'the two goddesses' instead of being individually named.

In some representations of Persephone, she is holding a pomegranate, which is a nod to her most famous myth, and one of the explanations for the changing seasons. Hades, the ruler of the Underworld, wanted to marry Persephone. So while Persephone was gathering flowers with her maidens, she wandered from the rest of them and became enthralled by a vibrant flower, which was commonly believed to be the narcissus flower.

In her distraction, Hades rose from the Underworld in his four-horse chariot, snatched her, and ferried her away to be his wife and queen.

Hecate and Helios told the distraught Demeter what had happened to her daughter. She wandered aimlessly in search of Persephone, neglecting her duties and causing the earth to become barren, without any good harvest for the mortals. It was, essentially, a bleak and never-ending winter, and was causing the people to die of famine.

Zeus intervened, and sent Hermes to the Underworld to return Persephone to Demeter so that she wouldn't be sad anymore. Hermes was successful, but did not get there in time before Persephone had eaten pomegranate seeds that had been grown in the Underworld. Some legends say she ate merely one seed, symbolizing the season of winter – some say she ate six seeds, which would represent six months. Either way, it meant that she had to remain in the Underworld for a certain amount of time every year. This developed into the myth that

explained the changing seasons, for whenever Persephone was in the Underworld, Demeter was too sad to allow the land to be fertile and grow plants. However, when Persephone returned, Demeter was happy enough to allow light and warmth to replenish the earth and allow it to become fertile once more.

Most of the myths including Persephone involves her in the Underworld. Adonis was a handsome young man that both Persephone and Aphrodite fell in love with. They couldn't agree between them who deserved him more, so Zeus bade Adonis spend six months with Persephone in the Underworld, and six months with Aphrodite. However, Adonis loved Aphrodite more and refused to go back to Persephone. Persephone was so angered by this that she sent a wild boar to kill Adonis. He

died in Aphrodite's arms and turned into the anemone flower.

Persephone didn't have any children with Hades, but she didn't mind Hades having dalliances with other beings. One of the few exceptions was the nymph Minthe, who was thought to be a mistress of Hades prior to Persephone's abduction. Minthe boasted that she was more beautiful than Persephone, and would win Hades back, so Persephone transformed Minthe into the mint plant to ensure that it would never happen.

Persephone was not simply a conquest and trophy wife of Hades in the Underworld. She had a large amount of authority and was often sought as an ally or helper by various heroes, and had the power to make decisions on behalf of Hades.

Persephone allowed Orpheus to leave with Eurydice, and permitted Heracles to take Cerberus as well. She also allowed Sysiphus to return to his wife, and agreed that Admetus and Alcestis could swap souls. She it was who granted Tiresias the ability to retain his intelligence in the Underworld.

Aside from her routine ventures to the surface due to the arrangement with Zeus and Demeter, Persephone is only said to leave the Underworld once: Pirithous, the king of the Lapiths, attempted to abduct her with the help of Theseus. The plan failed, and Pirithous was bound to a chair in Hades forever as punishment.

LEFT: Red figure bell crater. Bowl for mixing wine and water. Persephone on left being guided back to earth by Hermes. Demeter on the right waits to receive her daughter.

ABOVE: Rape of Persephone. Marble statue by Gian Lorenzo Bernini.

BELOW: Hades with his horse-drawn chariot to take Persephone to the underworld. By Walter Crane.

OPPOSITE: Earthenware head of Persephone from Sicily, Italy, circa 420 BC.

Prometheus, though a Titan, was one of the only Titans to defect to the side of Zeus during the Titanomachy – the war between Zeus and his siblings, and the ruling order of the Titans led by Cronus.

PROMETHEUS

ABOVE: Prometheus sitting on a rock, thoughtfully holds the body of a man he has molded from clay. Painting by Otto Greiner 1909.

Prometheus was said to have foreseen the outcome of the war and so he decided not to fight with the rest of the Titans.

After the war, Zeus bestowed on Prometheus the important role of bringing life to the earth. He crafted men out of clay, into which Zeus breathed life. Prometheus and Epimetheus were also responsible for giving living creatures characteristics that the other Greek gods and goddesses had manufactured. However, Epimetheus, whose name translates to 'afterthought', used up all the characteristics before getting to man, so Prometheus raided the workshops of the gods and found wisdom and reason, which he allocated to mankind.

He knew this action would anger Zeus, so he promised he would teach man how to make sacrifices to the gods. He had man divide up a prime bull, separating the parts into two piles; one pile had all the choice cuts, while the other was just bones and other unusable parts of the animal. Prometheus made the second pile look more appealing, and Zeus chose the second pile, meaning that all future sacrifices would be the second-best parts of an animal when offered to the gods.

Most famously, Prometheus is known as giving mankind the gift of fire. After his trick with the bull, Zeus was angry and removed fire from mankind. Prometheus didn't want his creations to suffer, so he again raided the workshops of the gods and stole a fennel stalk that contained an ember of fire from Hephaestus. He returned to earth with this stalk and showed man how to make fire so that man could not be deprived of it again.

In retribution, Zeus had Hephaestus construct Pandora from clay and gifted her to Epimetheus. When Pandora opened her famous box, mankind was doomed to suffer all the evil things that escaped from it, so Zeus continued to punish the creations of Prometheus.

After mankind was suitably punished, Zeus turned his attention to Prometheus once again. The final straw for Zeus was that Prometheus refused to tell Zeus about his prophesied downfall, so Zeus condemned Prometheus to an eternal punishment. Prometheus was chained to an unmovable rock in the Caucasus mountains with unbreakable chains. Every day, a giant eagle would come and devour the liver of Prometheus in front of him, and every night the liver would regrow so that Prometheus would suffer the new torment every single day.

Prometheus was finally released by Heracles, who needed his assistance and therefore shot

the eagle when it came on its daily mission. Heracles then released Prometheus from his chains, and Prometheus agreed to tell Zeus about the prophecy of his downfall in payment for being released.

Prometheus eventually partnered Pronoia, an Oceanid nymph, with whom he had a son. Deucalion was similarly called the 'Savior of Man', as Prometheus warned Deucalion when the great flood was coming. Before Zeus could send forth the flood water, Prometheus told Deucalion to build a boat, where he and Pyrrha (the daughter of Epimetheus and Pandora), would survive the great flood and repopulate the world.

Prometheus chained to a rock, being tortured by an eagle who comes everyday to feast on Prometheus' liver. Painting by Salvator Rosa, circa 1646 - 48.

THE CENTAURS

Centaurs (or Kentauroi) are creatures that are half man, half horse. They inhabited the mountains and forest of Thessaly and worshiped the god of wine, Dionysus. They were said to be primal, bestial creatures, symbolizing the war between the civilized and animal self.

There are several different myths concerning the creation of Centaurs. One is that Centaurus, the child of King Ixion, mated with the cloud nymph Nephele. Another is that Ixion himself mated with Nephele, and a different myth is that Centaurus mated with the Magnesian mares. This explains why Centaurs were half man and half horse.

They lived in their caves on Mount Pelion, where the daughters of the immortal centaur Chiron nursed them. Centaurs were known to be rowdy, boisterous, and savage creatures.

The Centauromachy is the name of the great battle which almost destroyed their entire race. King Pirithous, their half-brother, invited them to attend his wedding to Hippodamia. Spurred by wine, the centaurs tried to carry off the bride as well as many of the female guests. Thus prompting the hero Theseus, who was also in attendance and very fond of Pirithous, to act in the bride's honor. Theseus reached for an ancient bowl near him and managed to smash it in the face of the centaur who had made off with Hippodamia. The blow cracked open the

centaur's skull and he was one of many centaurs to die at the hands of Theseus. Without this substantial help, the King and his allies would have probably fallen to the brutal warriors.

Of the centaurs, Chiron is perhaps the best known. He was incredibly wise, and was a tutor and advisor for heroes such as Heracles, Achilles, and Jason. He was the son of Philyra and Cronus, and married the nymph Chariklo. He gifted Achilles a spear made of ash trees from Mount Pelion, which Achilles would go on to use during the Trojan War. Chiron was one of the only centaurs who resisted the call of wine and bestial activities, as he was much wiser than his brethren and had a different lineage.

Chiron was eventually wounded by Heracles with a poisoned arrow. This murder was an accident. It happened during a skirmish that broke out while a tribe of centaurs in the western Peloponnese hosted Heracles during one of his required labors. One centaur, Pholos, and Heracles were drinking together and began to fight due to the effects of the wine. Pholos was killed by a poisoned arrow in the same chaotic battle. Chiron was immortal, and therefore could not die, but endured incredible pain. He volunteered to take the place of Prometheus when Heracles asked for Prometheus to be freed. Chiron died free from the pain of the poison.

Centaurs often were used as a cautionary tale for the Greeks against the effects of wine and additional primal urges, portrayed as uncivilized and barbaric despite characters like Chiron. They served as symbols to epitomize the battle between civilization and barbarianism prevalent in Greek mythology.

ABOVE: Battle between Lapiths and Centaurs, painted by Piero di Cosimo, circa 1500-1515. This is probably part of a bench or chest in a Florentine palace.

LEFT: A bronze statue of a centaur pointing toward the heavens.

OPPOSITE TOP: Terracotta jar showing the centaur Pholos and Heracles between Iolaos and Hermes.

OPPOSITE BOTTOM: Ancient Roman sarcophagus showing a battle with mortals and centaurs.

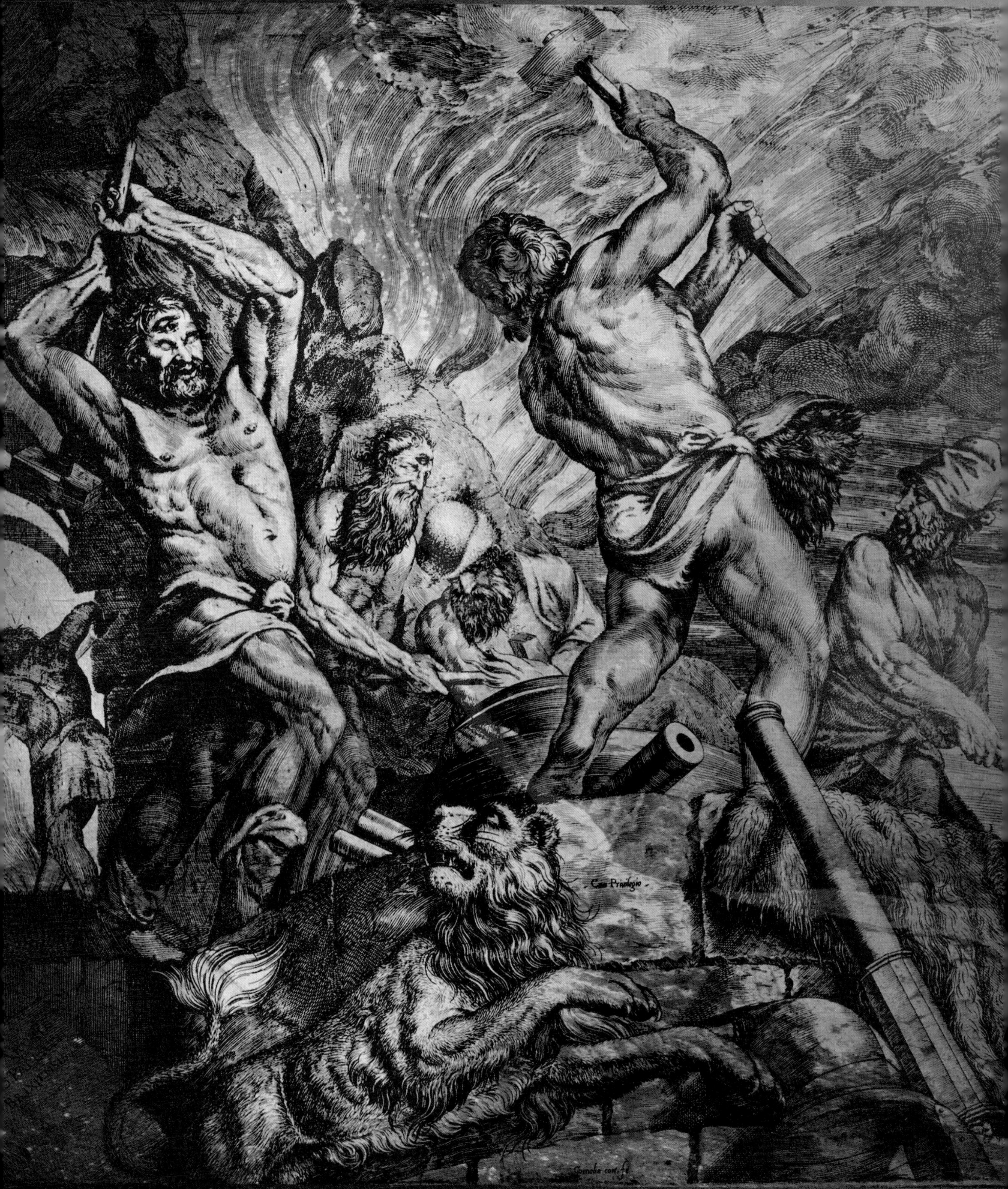

THE CYCLOPES

The Cyclopes (Cyclops) were one-eyed giants known for their great strength.

The original three Cyclopes were Arges, Steropes, and Brontes, and were all blacksmiths. They were the sons of Uranus and Gaia, and brothers of the Hecatonchires and the Titans. They were one of the races who sided with Zeus during the Titanomachy, and were released from the Underworld by Zeus after being imprisoned by Cronus. They forged thunderbolts for Zeus for use during the great battle. They were skilled metalworkers, and took up workmanship with Hephaestus in the heart of the volcano Etna.

The original Cyclopes, children of Uranus and Gaia, were released by Zeus at the urging of Gaia, who told Zeus that he would not be able to overthrow Cronus without their help. They forged the thunderbolts for Zeus, as well as a trident for Poseidon, and a helmet of invisibility for Hades. After the war, the Cyclopes continued their work, going on to forge armor for Athena and a chariot for Ares. It was also said that they were responsible for the building of the immense walls of Tiryns and the Lion Gate at Mycenae.

These three original Cyclopes eventually met their end at the hands of the Olympian gods. Arges was killed by Hermes while guarding Io from Zeus, and Apollo killed Steropes and Brontes as revenge for the death of his son, Asclepius. Although the Cyclopes had only forged the thunderbolt which Zeus threw at Asclepius, Apollo believed that they were responsible for the death of his son and took his revenge.

During later legends, the Cyclopes were described as dim-witted and violent one-eyed shepherds. These Cyclopes were not blacksmiths, nor were they portrayed as being intelligent or obedient. The most famous of these was the man-eating Polyphemus, who was a shepherd who was tricked and blinded by Odysseus.

Prior to this encounter which led to him being blinded by Odysseus, Polyphemus had fallen in love with Galatea, a beautiful nymph. She rejected his overtures in favor of Acis, who was the son of Faunus and the river nymph Symaethis. In a rage, Polyphemus killed Acis by throwing him on a gigantic rock, causing his blood to gush and form a stream that bears his name to this day.

Odysseus encountered Polyphemus on the island of the Cyclopes, where they were said to live in the later legends. Poseidon was the father of Polyphemus, and decided that his brutish son would be able to kill the hero. Poseidon held a grudge against Odysseus and wanted to prevent him from returning to Ithaca.

Polyphemus ate six of Odysseus's men, so the cunning Odysseus had to devise an escape plan or else risk the lives of the rest of his crew. He got Polyphemus drunk and blinded him in his sleep. Then he told his men to hide under the bellies of the sheep of Polyphemus, who being blinded was unable to tell the difference between the sheep and the men. Odysseus smuggled his crew out of the cave and escaped the Cyclops.

ABOVE: A stone head of a cyclopes, dated first century AD.

OPPOSITE: Cyclops forge heavenly artillery for Zeus and other gods. *Forge of the Cyclopes* by Cornelis Cort 1572.

BELOW: Polyphemus counts his sheep as they leave his cave to go and graze all day. Odysseus's men strap themselves to the under-belly of the sheep to escape the cave and Polyphemus.

THE FATES

The Fates, also known as the Moirai, are three goddesses who weave threads into tapestries that follow the events and lives of mortals.

They are Clotho the Spinner, Lachesis the Allotter, and Atropos the Inflexible. In older myths they are said to be the daughters of Nyx, however in more recent ones they are said to be the daughters of Zeus and Themis, or Ananke, also known as 'Necessity'.

The Fates were immensely powerful, to the point where not even Zeus could argue their judgements. They were commonly portrayed as three women, sometimes as 'handsome', and sometimes as old and ugly hag-like women. Each of them had a different task in spinning the thread of a mortal. Clotho spun the thread, Lachesis measured its length, and Atropos cut the thread.

The Fates rarely intervened when it came to the lives and deaths of mortals and gods, so they do not appear in many myths as a unit. Clotho often forced Aphrodite to sleep with other gods. The Fates killed the Titan Typhon, and restored Pelops back to life after he was torn to pieces and cooked by his father Tantalus.

In one instance where the Fates spoke to a mortal, they warned Althaea that her son, Meleager, would only live until a log, which was currently burning in the hearth, turned to ash. Wanting to save her son, Althaea removed the log and hid it away. After a fight over a boar skin, Meleager murdered her brothers, his uncles. She threw the log into the fire, killing Meleager, and then killed herself out of despair.

The only time the Fates were deceived was by Apollo. Apollo learned that his favorite, Admetus, was destined to die, and so he got the Fates drunk and bargained with them to spare the life of Admetus, if he could find someone to take his place. The Fates agreed, but Apollo failed to find a replacement. Alcestis, wife of Admetus, volunteered in order to save the life of her husband. In some versions of the myth, Alcestis was the one who organized the trade originally instead of Apollo.

atropos

lachesis

clotho

THIS PAGE: This tapestry is called The Triumph of Death, or, The Three Fates. It shows Clotho, Lachesis and Atropos in triumph, standing over the fallen body of Chastity.

OPPOSITE TOP RIGHT: Marble statue of Atropos cutting the thread.

OPPOSITE MIDDLE: Bronze statue of Clotho the spinner.

OPPOSITE BOTTOM: Painting of Lachesis measuring thread.

THE FURIES

The Furies (Erinyes) are a group of winged female deities that mercilessly chased and tormented those who committed grievous moral crimes. They were born from the blood of Uranus when Cronus castrated him.

ABOVE: The marble head of one of the Furies sleeping.

MAIN IMAGE: This is a shrine of Erinyes, also known as the Furies.

Some authors wrote that they were the children of Hades and Persephone, some said they were daughters of Nyx (Night), and others that they were the children of Earth and Darkness.

They were demonic creatures who flew endlessly after their prey, similar to portrayals of harpies. They were able to transform, and had black skin covered by black dresses. They

were said to have frightening and horrific faces and snakes for hair, similar to the Gorgon Medusa. Their breath was poisonous, and they foamed at the mouth which would also poison their prey when they shrieked at them. They could breathe fire, spread illnesses, and prevent plants from growing naturally.

The primary duty of the Furies was to stalk and harass mercilessly, those who had committed crimes against their families or rulers. Specifically, children who had defied or wronged their parents. They pursued and punished murderers; those who were consumed with hatred or malice, and those that had committed perjury. They also punished those who went against the natural order of things, including mortals who would steal chicks from bird's nests.

The Furies were used as a narrative for the ancient Greeks to symbolize remorse and guilt which plagued those who had committed injustices, or a criminal act which led to their destruction. They were a metaphor for the

ABOVE: Orestes pursued by the Furies.
John Singer Sargent, 1921.

divine eye of justice which sees everything, and punishes wrongdoers. No one was safe from the wrath of the Furies.

Euripides named three Furies: Alecto (rage and mania) who punished moral crimes such as anger towards others, Tisiphone (revenge to killings) who targeted murderers especially, and Megaera (hatred and envy) who specifically punished marital infidelity. They were similar in power to Nemesis, except that the Furies punished crimes against mortals only, whereas Nemesis had the power to punish crimes against the gods.

In the Aeneid, Tisiphone is named as a guard of the gates of Tartarus. In the Iliad the Furies pursued the god Ares because he helped the Trojans against the wishes of his mother, Hera. Similarly, Telemachus was threatened with the wrath of the Furies if he chose to drive his mother Penelope away from their home. Meleager's mother invoked the Furies against Meleager for killing her brothers.

The Furies served as vigilantes in many Greek works, such as the myths of Orestes and Oedipus. Oedipus hadn't intended to kill his father, however he was found guilty of the crime of patricide and was therefore pursued by the Furies. Orestes, the son of Agamemnon and Clytemnestra, was persecuted by the Furies for the murder of his mother.

The Furies, on occasion, lost the reputation of being merciless and brutal hags pursuing wrongdoers. In the instance of mortals who were held as figures of high moral and ethical character, the Furies transformed into the Eumenides: benevolent deities. Their role was to protect foreign visitors and beggars. They would also remove negative manifestations such as destruction, disease, danger, drought, or harmful winds from a man or country. Instead they would bring euphoria, health, and prosperity to those deemed worthy of their more beneficial manifestation.

THE GIANTS

The Gigantomachy, or "War of the Giants", was a continuation of the Titanomachy. After Zeus defeated Cronus and his allies, he sealed away the Titans and their allies in Tartarus so that they wouldn't be able to rise up against him again.

LEFT: This relief shows Athena on the left, and the Giants portrayed as Tritons, all in battle with each other. Made in the Roman period, 2nd century AD.

BELOW: Gigantomachy scene: Poseidon fighting Polybotes. 475-470 BC.

BOTTOM: This depicts Heracles killing Alcyonea, holding his head back and thrusting his sword into his side.

OPPOSITE: An epic battle of the Giants. In the middle a lion attacks one of the soldiers.

The Giants were terrifying creatures, notable for their incredible size and strength. The first Giants were the Hecatonchires and Cyclopes, who were imprisoned by Uranus in Tartarus during the empire of the Titans. When Cronus defeated Uranus and usurped him, he refused to release the captive Giants. When Zeus declared war during the Titanomachy, he went to Tartarus to free the Hecatonchires and Cyclopes, who proceeded to help him win the war. They then became the guards of the Titans that Zeus imprisoned in Tartarus after the war.

Gaia, who was mother of Cronus and grandmother of Zeus, was so upset by the behavior of Zeus that she created more Giants, who began to wage war against the new gods of Olympus.

The gods of Olympus consulted an Oracle, who told them that the Giants could not be defeated by any of the gods, but that only mortal hands could slay them. Once he learned this, Zeus sent for his demigod Heracles. Gaia attempted to make a potion to protect the Giants so that mortals couldn't slay them, but Zeus intervened and destroyed the potion before she could give it to the Giants.

Heracles managed to slay all the Giants by using arrows dipped in poison from the Hydra of Lerna. Specifically, Heracles attacked Alcyoneus, piercing him with a poisoned arrow, and dragged the Giant out of his homeland so that Heracles could kill him. Another adaptation says that Heracles killed the Giant by breaking his neck with his bare hands.

The Giants were eventually defeated: killed by Heracles or by other allies of Zeus.

There were three monsters in Greek mythology labeled as the Gorgons. They were the daughters of Echidna and Typhon, the mother and father of all monsters: Stheno, Euryale, and the most famous Gorgon, Medusa.

THE GORGONS

ABOVE: A fragment with an ornate design, comprising a Gorgon mask, a gold-colored vase, and a bird with outspread wings. This type of painting was found on many walls in Pompeii.

Medusa was the only one of the three who was not immortal. Medusa was considered to be the child of Phorkys and Keto rather than Echidna and Typhon.

The Gorgons were notoriously ugly, their hair was made of snakes, and anyone who gazed into their eyes would be instantly turned to stone.

Medusa was not originally a hideous Gorgon, but had been a beautiful mortal until she brought the wrath of Athena upon herself. This was as a result of her pride and an ill-fated affair with Poseidon. After her transformation, Medusa was depicted as having golden wings and a bronze head, with boar-like tusks and fanged teeth. Her hair was like other Gorgons, and made of a mass of writhing snakes.

Poseidon was unable to resist Medusa before her transformation, for she was said to have a beautiful face and that her hair was her finest feature. Poseidon impregnated Medusa inside Athena's temple, which enraged the virgin goddess, prompting her to turn Medusa into a monster like her sisters. Whether or not the affair with Poseidon was consensual or not has been a matter of interpretation for a number of years, and Athena's actions have been construed as merciful in some interpretations, so that Medusa would not receive unwanted affections ever again.

Polydectes, the king of Seriphos at the time, wanted to get rid of the hero Perseus, and so sent him on a quest to bring him the head of Medusa. Perseus set off on this quest and, with the help of Athena and Hermes, reached the land of the Gorgons on the rocky island of Sarpedon. He used the reflection in Athena's bronze shield so that he wouldn't look at Medusa directly, and killed her by cutting off her head while she slept.

Medusa was still pregnant by Poseidon at the time of her death, and when Perseus severed her head, Chrysaor and Pegasus sprang from

the neck of Medusa. Her Gorgon sisters were awoken by the noise the children made. They attempted to kill Perseus in revenge, but Perseus had Hades' helmet of invisibility and the winged sandals of Hermes, and managed to escape.

Perseus took the head of Medusa back to Seriphos, and turned Polydectes and all of his followers to stone. He made them look into her eyes, which still held that power even after her death. Perseus then gave Athena the head and she collected the blood of Medusa. This she gave to Asclepius, who would use blood from different sides of Medusa to take the lives of people, or raise them from the dead.

LEFT: Marble statue of Perseus holding the Head of Medusa which he has just cut off. 18th century copy from original version in the Vatican.

BELOW: Medusa's head, painted by Caravaggio in 1597. It depicts the exact moment that Perseus cuts off her head. From her neck spurts blood, while the snakes on her head writhe and coil.

The rest of Medusa's blood was given to Athena's adopted son Erichthonius – there were two drops inside a vial. One drop was said to be a cure-all, the other drop was a deadly poison.

Athena then took a single lock of Medusa's hair and kept it in a bronze jar, which she gave to Heracles. He in turn gave it to the daughter of Cepheus, Sterope, as a means of protection for her home. Even though the lock of hair didn't have the same power as the Gorgon's gaze, and could not turn people into stone, it could strike fear into the heart of anyone who was unfortunate enough to look at it.

THE HYDRA

The Hydra was another child of Echidna and Typhon, and was an immortal creature who lived in the swamps around Lake Lerna. It was a giant snake-like creature with many heads, supported by long necks which could strike an enemy in any direction. The Hydra was also commonly depicted with two tails.

ABOVE: *Hercules and the Hydra*, painted by John Singer Sargent, 1921. Hercules was the Roman name for Heracles.

OPPOSITE TOP: *Hercules and the Hydra of Lerna*, by Gustave Moreau, 1876.

OPPOSITE BOTTOM: A statue of Heracles slaying the Hydra, 17th century.

It was a ferocious and vicious creature, which had been trained by Hera to attack anything it came across. It plagued the country around Lake Lerna, devouring hundreds of civilians and ravaging the surrounding villages. It was however also known to be very lazy, and would only emerge from its cave if hungry or goaded.

The Hydra's blood was known to be poisonous, and some brave souls that wandered too close could die simply from smelling its foul breath. Even after the Hydra was killed, its blood was used as a potent poison for many weapons. The Hydra was also capable of regeneration on top of being immortal; one of its heads was immortal and protected by the many others. If any of the mortal heads were cut off, two or more would sprout in its place. Only by cutting off the immortal head could the monster be slain.

The Hydra was chosen by Hera to be one of the labors of Heracles. Hera had specifically adopted and raised the beast with the intention of killing Heracles. Heracles was proof of the infidelity of Zeus and the hated Heracles was growing into a great hero.

Heracles approached the swamp where the Hydra lived with his mouth and nose covered in thick fabric, so that he would be protected from the poisonous scent of the Hydra. He shot fiery arrows into the cave to draw the beast out, with great success. Heracles began cutting off the monster's heads as quickly as he could, but of course each severed head prompted more to grow in their place.

After a brief and intense battle, Heracles realized he would not be able to hack his way to the immortal head, so he called to Iolaus, his nephew, for aid. Iolaus brought a torch and cauterized the bloody stumps of the heads, so that new ones couldn't grow whenever Heracles cut one off. Observing that he was winning,

Hera tried to distract Heracles by sending a giant crab to strike him, but Heracles crushed the crab under his foot.

After successfully cutting off many of the heads and burning the bloody stumps, Heracles reached the immortal head and severed it with a golden sword, which had been given to him by Athena. He then buried the body of the Hydra under a large rock, finally crushing it. After killing the Hydra, Heracles harvested its poisonous blood and dipped some of his arrows in it. He used these poisoned arrows in future battles.

That wasn't the end of the Hydra which indirectly exacted its revenge on Heracles. Heracles used one of the poisoned arrows to kill the centaur Nessus. As Nessus lay dying, he told the wife of Heracles that his blood could be used as a love charm. This would make Heracles faithful to his wife for the rest of his days. In fact, since his blood was tainted by the Hydra's poison, the blood of Nessus became a weapon in its own right. The wife of Heracles dipped her husband's clothes in the centaur's blood. When Heracles wore the clothes, the Hydra's poison burned his flesh and killed him.

THE NYMPHS

The Nymphs in Greek mythology were minor goddesses, usually tied to various aspects of the natural world such as water, islands, trees, and mountains.

They were usually described as very beautiful and gracious, as well as shy around people, and so rarely appeared to humans. Nymphs were often the wives or lovers of gods or powerful kings, and while not quite immortal, had much longer lives than typical humans.

There were as many types of Nymphs as there were natural areas for them to live in. The Alseides were the spirits of groves and glens, the Auloniad Nymphs were associated with pastures and shepherds, Napaeae were Nymphs of dells, and Leimonides were Nymphs of meadows.

The most popular types of Nymphs to appear in legend were the water Nymphs. The ancient Greeks believed that all water on earth was connected, so all the water Nymphs could travel to each other's domains. Most of them stayed close to home, however, and could be identified by the type of water into which they were born. In many legends a single water Nymph could be attributed to many different types. The Oceanid, Nereid, and Naiad. The Titan Oceanus sired the first kind, and was said to have three thousand daughters. Poseidon's wife was a Nereid named Amphitrite.

The Naiads resided in streams, pools, fountains, and natural wells. They were the daughters of the river gods, and the nieces of the Oceanids. Every feeder stream, current, and curve in a larger river could have a single Naiad attributed to it. Because of their proximity to humans as freshwater Nymphs, the Naiads were much more inclined to interact with mortals.

There were fifty named Nereids, daughters of the primordial sea god Nereus. They were saltwater goddesses, specifically the Mediterranean Sea. They represented the sea's beauty and benefits, and were helpers of fisherman and sailors. They were often described as the kindest and most well-behaved of the Nymphs.

Dryads were nymphs of plants. Originally the term Dryad was only applied to Nymphs who were the spirits of oak trees, but this took on a broader definition in later tales. There were also the Anthousai, for flowers; the Ampeloi, for grape vines; and the Hamadryads, for oak trees. The Hamadryads were sedentary and rarely strayed from their trees, which made the Greeks take great care when cutting down trees or traversing forest. They had to make sure not to destroy a tree that was being inhabited by a Dryad.

It was dangerous to enter the forest, as muddying a stream or breaking a branch could anger the Nymph that lived there. Similarly, interrupting a group of Dryads that were dancing or bathing could incite their wrath.

Some Dryads were said to be the ancestors of mankind. The Meliae were Oread-nymphs of the mountain ash tree. They were the children of Gaia and were wives of the Silver Race of Man, and mothers of the Bronze – the third generation of mankind.

ABOVE: Ancient relief carving depicting a fight between nymph and a satyr.

OPPOSITE: Cave of the Storm Nymphs showing the nymph on the left playing a scallop-shell lyre. The other nymphs await more treasure from the battered ship, to be swept into the cave. Edward Poynter 1903.

ABOVE: A passing shepherd has discovered a sleeping nymph, the nymph is a vision of innocent youth.

ABOVE RIGHT: The constellation of Orion showing how the stars make up the shape of the giant, Orion, who relentlessy chased the Seven Sisters.

In two types of stories, women were magically transformed into trees. Daphne was a water Nymph who was being pursued by Apollo, and transformed herself into a laurel tree to escape his advances. Escaping the lust of a man or god was a common reason for such transformations. Another was that they were so overcome by emotion that the gods took pity on them, and turned them into a tree to end their suffering.

Some Nymphs lived in the air and the skies, and were known as the Celestial Nymphs. The Aurae were air Nymphs, living in gentle breezes. These were separate from the four winds, which were personified by four gods or four swift horses and were often described as strong and violent. The Asteriae were the second type of Celestial Nymphs and inhabited the stars.

There were three groups of Asteriae, categorized by constellations. The Hyades were thought to bring rain, as their appearance in the sky happened around the start of the rainy season in Greece. The Pleiades, or the Seven Sisters, were another group, and were the daughters of Atlas.

Other categories of Nymphs include minor goddesses that fit into the Nymph archetype, but are not explicitly part of the original lineage of Nymphs. They are: the Hecaterides, the mothers of satyrs and companions of Dionysus; the Maenads; the Lenai, who were goddesses of the wine press; the Cabeirides who presided over the orgiastic rites of Samothracian Mysteries; the Melissae, who were Nymphs of hives and beekeeping; the Epimelides, the apple orchard Nymphs and the protectors of sheep and goats. Many of these Nymph groups are known for their association with Dionysus.

The categories of Nymphs were fluid and changing, and one Nymph could take many forms or change roles depending on her circumstances.

Popular recurring characters in Greek mythology were the Nymphs known as the Seven Sisters. They were nurses to Dionysus as an infant after his mother's death, and several became the lovers of Olympian gods. Maia was one such, who became the mother of Hermes.

The Seven Sisters became the subject of lust from the giant, Orion, who pursued them

relentlessly since their father, Atlas, couldn't protect them as he was busy holding up the sky. The Sisters threw themselves from a high cliff to escape Orion, and Zeus turned them into birds to save their lives. He then transformed them into stars, as thanks for their service to Dionysus and to appease Atlas, and they formed a constellation above the head of Atlas. When Orion became a constellation, they remained forever out of his reach.

Another group of Dryads, the Hesperides, were a second set of daughters by Atlas. One of the tasks of Heracles was to steal a golden apple from their garden. The apples were a gift from Hera to whom they were fiercely loyal, and were closely guarded by the Hesperides. This set them apart from other Dryads who usually were associated with Dionysus or Artemis.

Only two groups of Nymphs resided in the Underworld – the Lampades. They were torch bearers and served Hecate, the goddess of witchcraft. They had been given to Hecate by Zeus as thanks for her services in the war with

the Titans. The Lampades were the only sinister Nymphs, and it was said that madness would come to anyone who touched their torches.

There were Naiads residing in the Underworld; Styx and Orphne. Styx was the personification of her river, whereas Orphne signified the darkness in the water of a river. These two Nymphs were the only natives, the others had been given as gifts, or forced to live in the Underworld.

Minthe was one such Dryad, who was one of the lovers of Hades. She willingly entered the Underworld, but Demeter turned her into the mint plant after Minthe taunted her. Leuce was a Dryad of the poplar tree who was abducted by Hades and lived the rest of her life in the Underworld.

All Nymphs are most famously remembered for being beautiful, graceful, and the lovers of gods, as well as mothers to demigods and heroes. In Greek culture, they were everywhere and forces to be respected in all aspects of nature.

ABOVE: The seven daughters of Atlas, after being saved by Zeus and transformed into stars, forever out of the reach of Orion who had been pursuing them.

BELOW: A Napaea, a nymph who lives in caves and valleys, sits with a bunch of meadow flowers near a meadow and looks out over a valley.

4
MORTALS

MORTALS

Greek mythology does not confine itself to the gods and supernatural beings, it includes mortals who have a significant place in the legends.

Heracles had to perform twelve seemingly impossible labors for King Eurystheus, and was later worshipped as a god for his accomplishment. Pandora was the first woman and her curiosity brought evil to mankind. Pygmalion was the king who fell in love with an ivory statue, and King Midas turned everything he touched to gold. Ganymede was the beautiful Trojan prince who became cupbearer to the gods and Narcissus fell in love with his own reflection. Arachne the weaver was so pleased with her fine cloth that she was turned into a spider because of her arrogance.

Generally, when mortals were involved with the gods, it ended unhappily for the mortals.

A detail of a cabinet depicting the heroic deeds of Heracles. Here we see him performing the second labor for King Eurystheus – to slay the nine-headed Lernaean Hydra. The Hydra was a fire-breathing monster, when one head was cut off, two would grow in its place. It had been sent by Hera.

ACHILLES

Achilles was one of the most famous of the Ancient Greek heroes, his legacy lasting even to this day with an 'Achilles Heel' being a synonymous term for someone's only weakness.

ABOVE RIGHT: Marble statue of Achilles.

ABOVE: A coin with the head of Achilles dated 4th century BC.

OPPOSITE: *Thetis dipping the infant Achilles into the river Styx.* Peter Paul Rubens.

Thetis, goddess of the sea, was loved by both Poseidon and Zeus. Themis and Prometheus told them of a prophecy that Thetis would bear a princely son, who would wield a weapon more powerful than a thunderbolt or trident. As a result of this warning, Peleus was chosen to be the husband of Thetis because he was known to be extremely pious, but more importantly, he was a mortal, which meant that he would be unable to sire a god.

A second prophecy from Themis told that the son of Thetis would either live for a long time and die in obscurity, or that he would die the death of a glorious warrior. As an immortal, Thetis wished for a long life for her son and desiring to protect him from harm, she held Achilles by the heel, and dipped him in the waters of the Styx. This would protect him and make him invulnerable to harm.

Thetis would also bathe the baby Achilles in ambrosia and burn away his mortality every night, holding parts of him by the fire in an attempt to cleanse him. She did this until Peleus found her and bade her stop. She was so offended, that she left Peleus and went back to the sea to live with her sister Nereids.

Achilles grew up on Mount Pelion, where the wise centaur Chiron was his mentor for many years, teaching him to hunt and play music. By the time Achilles returned to his father, he already had the bearing of a hero, and was destined for greatness.

To protect her son from being involved in the Trojan War, Thetis disguised Achilles as a girl, living in a foreign court. Odysseus determined that the Greeks would lose the war without the help of Achilles and discovered him living at the Court of Lycomedes. It was here that Odysseus tricked Achilles into revealing his true identity.

Another version of this myth says that Odysseus had disguised himself as a peddler in possession of a spear and only Achilles or 'Pyrrha' took interest, which revealed his true identity.

ABOVE: *The education of Achilles*, painted by Eugène Delacroix circa 1862.

Achilles joined the army with a fleet of 50 ships, each of which carried 50 men, which were called the Myrmidons. The fleet became lost, and landed in Mysia, which was ruled by Telephus, one of the sons of Heracles. The army of Telephus managed to drive them away, but not before Achilles had wounded Telephus. An oracle told Telephus that only the person who could heal the wound was the one who had inflicted it, so Telephus asked Achilles to heal him. In return, he gave the Greeks directions on how to reach Troy.

There were more vicissitudes to come. Agamemnon had killed one of the sacred deer of Artemis. She in fury held back the winds from the fleet until she was offered a human sacrifice. Agamemnon told his daughter Iphigenia that she was to marry Achilles at Aulius, where the deer had been killed. Achilles discovered that Agamemnon intended his daughter to be sacrificed and he attempted to save her but without success. Eventually Iphigenia agreed to be sacrificed, and the winds changed, allowing the Greeks to set sail again. However, the relationship between Agamemnon and Achilles had soured.

The first island they landed on was Tenedos. Against the advice of his mother, Achilles killed the king, Tenes. Unfortunately for Achilles, the father of Tenes was Apollo, who swore that he would have his revenge on the Greek hero.

In the tenth year of the Trojan War, Agamemnon had enslaved Chryseis. Her father was a priest of Apollo and begged the god to help him. Apollo sent a plague to the Greek forces, until Agamemnon agreed to return Chryseis. This would be in exchange for a woman, Briseis, who was a prize of Achilles. Achilles was so furious at Agamemnon for this continued show of dishonor that he left the battlefield and refused to take up arms in aid of the Greeks. He even asked Thetis, his mother, to petition Zeus to help the Trojans so that Agamemnon and the Greeks would realize the consequences of dishonoring their greatest warrior.

Zeus agreed, allowing the Trojans enough strength and aid to help them to push the Greeks back from Troy and to their ships. Agamemnon, realizing his mistake in angering Achilles, sent Odysseus with apologies and gifts to entreat Achilles to return to battle. Achilles still refused.

Patroclus, who was the dearest and most beloved friend of Achilles, feared that the Greeks would lose the war, and that many of their friends would die. He asked for the armor of Achilles and donned it. Disguising himself as the warrior, he led an attack on the Trojans. However, after pressing onward, he fell to Hector during the battle.

Achilles was so distraught by death of Patroclus, that it convinced him to take up arms again, as he was determined to kill Hector in revenge. He put on new armor that was made by Hephaestus, tracked down Hector, and killed him in a duel. He then attached the body of Hector to his chariot and rode around the city of Troy for twelve days. Hector's father begged for his son's body back with such sincerity, that Achilles was moved to return the body for burial.

The end prophecy for Achilles came to pass soon after. Hector was one of Troy's best soldiers, and after his death, Paris took up arms and fought Achilles, piercing his heel with an arrow. He hit the only part of Achilles that was vulnerable to injury. Whether the arrow was poisoned or not is a matter of debate, but it was certainly guided by Apollo, who still sought revenge against Achilles, and knew where to strike him.

In the Odyssey, Odysseus encountered the ghost of Achilles as a minor ruler of the dead in the underworld. While Odysseus admired Achilles for such a station, Achilles was not so happy and said he would rather be a servant and alive, than a king among the dead.

ABOVE: A plate showing Paris killing Achilles, circa 1525.

BELOW: The side of this terracotta pot shows Achilles fighting in the Trojan war with his spear and shield.

The Amazons were a race of warrior women, descended from Ares, the god of War. They were known for their strength, pride, and courage, often keeping to themselves.

THE AMAZONS

ABOVE: A marble statue of Penthesilea, one of the queens of the Amazons. Made by by Gabriel-Vital Dubray, 1862.

One of their Queens was Hippolyta, to whom Ares gave a magical golden belt that would grant her the title of Queen of the Amazons. Intermarriage with other tribes was allowed, as there were no men among the Amazons, but male children were either killed, sent back to live with their fathers, or left to fend for themselves.

Though the Amazons were a self-contained and independent people, they were often incorporated into stories of heroes. Heracles famously sailed to their land to ask Queen Hippolyta for her belt, which was his ninth labor. She agreed to meet him in secret on his ship, where he told her his story. She was so moved by his desire to atone and complete his labors that she agreed to give him the belt for the purpose of finishing his ninth task.

This was meant to be a secret meeting because Hera was trying vengefully to thwart Heracles at every turn. She disguised herself as an Amazonian and told them that Heracles intended to trick them and kidnap Hippolyta. Furious, the Amazons swarmed the ship, and while Hippolyta tried to calm them, they wouldn't listen. Heracles knew he didn't have time, so he took the belt, put Hippolyta safely off his ship, and set sail, leaving her wondering if her decision had been the right one.

Theseus was another hero who visited Hippolyta after slaying the minotaur. Hippolyta brought gifts for him, and held a great feast in his honor. The next morning, she boarded his ship to meet him, and Theseus became enamored of her. He proposed to her, promising her the title of Queen of Athens, with all the jewels in the world, and glory and riches.

Hippolyta declined, as she had an obligation to her people. She didn't hear them secretly set sail while she was still on board, and when she tried to leave, he claimed her as his bride and sailed to Athens.

The Amazons were infuriated that their Queen had been stolen and immediately set sail for Athens in great numbers. Theseus had been planning a celebration in honor of his wedding, and was not aware of the impending attack which happened at night. Hippolyta was rescued and taken home by her Amazon sisters with the promise that they would be more wary of visitors in the future.

Penthesilea was another queen of the Amazons who became Queen after accidentally killing her sister Hippolyta, with a spear. Her reputation was that of a fierce warrior: she is credited with the invention of the battle axe.

She was also considered to be very wise and beautiful. However, she was so riddled with grief and regret that she wished for death, but the only honorable death she could have would be on the field of battle.

This was during the Trojan War. Penthesilea went with her army to fight and defend Troy. Some stories say that she sought absolution from King Priam for killing Hippolyta, some say she was boastful and said that she would kill the legendary hero Achilles, other say that she was simply a mercenary who accepted treasure for defending Troy.

When dawn came, Penthesilea donned the armor her father Ares had given her and set out onto the battlefield. It was the first battle after the truce which followed the death of Hector. Both sides had lost many soldiers. Penthesilea faced off against Ajax the Great, but neither could gain the advantage.

Ajax was then replaced by Achilles, who stepped up to fight the Amazon Queen. In a simple version of the story, Achilles pierced her armor with a spear and killed her. In a more complex version, and a less common one, Penthesilea lived up to her boast and killed Achilles. Achilles was then resurrected when Thetis begged Zeus to restore him, and the resurrected Achilles killed Penthesilea.

Achilles removed her helmet and was so taken by her beauty that he returned her body to Troy unmolested. This earned him the mockery of Thersites, who then gouged out the eyes of Penthesilea's corpse, prompting an angry Achilles to kill him.

ABOVE: *Hercules obtaining the girdle of Hippolyta*, painted by Nicolaes Knüpfer, first half of 17th century (Hercules was the Roman name for Heracles).

BELOW: *Departure of the Amazons*, painted by Claude Déruet, circa 1620s.

ARACHNE

In the first version of Arachne's myth, she was a skilled weaver and the daughter of a shepherd, who boasted so much of her skill that it angered Athena. Athena appeared and challenged Arachne to a contest.

BELOW: *Minerva and Arachne*, painted by René-Antoine Houasse, 1706.

Athena wove scenes depicting humans committing hubris and being punished by the gods, while Arachne wove scenes where the gods abused humans. Arachne's work was much better than Athena's, which infuriated Athena so much that she transformed Arachne into a spider and condemned her to weave for eternity.

In the second version, Athena depicted the contest between herself and Poseidon over who should be the patron deity of Athens. Arachne chose to weave a scene of the dalliances of Zeus with various mortal women – particularly those where he appeared to them in animal form. It was a crude homage to the King of the Gods, and while Athena acknowledged the skill of her adversary, she wanted Arachne to have more respect. She touched the forehead of Arachne and filled her with shame, causing Arachne to hang herself. Athena resurrected her and turned her into a spider so that she could continue to weave.

In the final version of this myth, Zeus presided over the contest, and declared Athena the victor. Whoever lost was never allowed to touch a loom or spindle again. Arachne was devastated by her loss and was no longer allowed to weave, so Athena transformed her into a spider out of pity, so that she could continue to weave without breaking her oath.

ARACHNE Also known as:
Arakhnê
Depending on the myth,
Arachne is either said to
be a talented weaver, or
the prideful daughter of a
shepherd who challenged
Athena to a contest.
There are three versions of
this myth.

THIS PAGE: Etching of *Arachne* by Otto
Henry Bacher 1884.

ABOVE: Pegasus the winged horse that Bellerophon eventually managed to tame.

OPPOSITE: A fresco from one of the walls at Pompeii, first century AD. It shows Bellerophon holding on to Pegasus, Athena is on the right with spear and shield.

The most famous accomplishments of Bellerophon were the taming of Pegasus, and the killing of the Chimera. Glaucus, having raised Bellerophon as his own child, instilled an interest in horses in the young boy early on.

BELLEROPHON

At this time there was a legendary winged horse named Pegasus, whom many had tried to tame. Bellerophon attempted to tame it many times, but was unsuccessful, so he turned to Polyeidus for help. Polyeidus was a Corinthian seer, who told Bellerophon to spend the night in the temple of Athena.

While there, Bellerophon dreamed that he was given a magical, golden horse bridle by a goddess. When he woke, the bridle lay beside him. He offered a sacrifice to Poseidon and Athena, before going to the field where Pegasus was grazing. However, he was still unable to tame the horse. His persistence was eventually rewarded and he succeeded in taming the legendary horse. He rode Pegasus to King Pittheaus to prove it, and was offered the hand of the King's daughter, Aethra, as a reward.

Unfortunately, before the wedding, Bellerophon accidentally killed someone and was banished from his home as punishment, so he was unable to marry Aethra.

After being banished, Bellerophon rode Pegasus to King Proetus, and asked for pardon. The king agreed and allowed Bellerophon to stay with him. Stheneboea, wife of Proetus, wanted to seduce Bellephoron, but he refused her advances. She was so insulted that she accused him of trying to seduce her, which enraged Proetus. Bellerophon was well-loved by the people, so he couldn't simply be punished or denigrated without causing upset. Similarly, harming a guest was a grievous sin against the Ancient Greek gods so Proetus wanted to avoid that.

He asked Bellerophon to send a letter to King Iobates, who was the father in law of Proetus. Bellerophon went to deliver the letter and was

BELLEROPHON Son of Poseidon and Eurynome, though he was raised by Eurynome's husband, Glaucus, the King of Corinth. Grandson of Sisyphus.
Sited as a common fable against pride and the damage which can be caused by conceit.
Married Philonoe, and had two sons, Hippolokhos and Isandros, and two daughters, Deidameia and Laodameia.
During his reign as king, he was loved and honored by his people.
Usually depicted as a young, strong, attractive man, either feeding or riding Pegasus. He is also often shown holding a magical spear which he used to conquer the Chimera.

ABOVE: *Pegasus and Bellerophon*, by Odilon Redon, circa 1888.

OPPOSITE: *Bellerophon Vanquishing the Chimera*, etching by Dominique Barrière, 1668.

His first quest was to kill the Chimera, which was a fire-breathing creature with the body and head of a lion, a second head of a goat, a snake for a tail, and sometimes reptilian wings. Bellerophon was able to kill the creature by shooting it from the back of Pegasus at a safe distance.

After that victory, Bellerophon was sent to kill an enemy tribe of Iobates, then the Amazons, against whom he was also victorious. Iobates then turned his own army against Bellerophon, who killed all but one soldier.

This finally proved to Iobates that the gods were on the side of Bellerophon, and he stopped trying to kill him. He apologized and offered Philonoe, his daughter, as a wife, which Bellerophon happily accepted.

Regarding Stheneboea, it's unclear whether Bellerophon took his revenge on her, by flying her up with Pegasus and then pushing her from a great height, or whether she took her own life after learning that Bellerophon had married her sister.

Bellerophon had four children with Philonoe and was happily married. However, his new life wasn't as satisfying for him as being a great hero and warrior. Restless and desiring further glory, he rode Pegasus up to Mount Olympus to ask the gods for another quest. Zeus wasn't happy with this, so he sent a gadfly to irritate Pegasus, which caused the horse to throw Bellerophon off its back mid-flight.

Bellerophon survived the fall, but he was permanently crippled and far from home. He spent the rest of his life wandering around searching for help. No one would help him because his fate was a result of the punishment of the gods, who they were not inclined to offend. He died alone, presumably from being unable to survive on his own with his injuries and without assistance.

warmly received, quickly making himself at home. The letter however contained details of his 'advances' on the daughter of Stheneboea. This caused Iobates to be upset with Bellerophon, but he was left in a predicament, where he could not harm a guest to his house.

So, he came up with a plan, and asked Bellerophon to embark on a series of quests, which were meant to be so dangerous that surely the young man would die. Bellerophon surprised him by easily completing these quests, as he was both a skilled archer and had the help of Pegasus, so he could win every battle he entered.

laudio Gillee Inu. Con licenza de sup · An · 1668·

CADMUS

The story of Cadmus began when Zeus abducted Europa, prompting her brothers and her cousin Thasus to set out on a quest to recover her.

This was, of course, an impossible task, since Zeus was a god and these men were mortal.

Nevertheless, they tried, and each ended up settling in various places. Phoenix ended his search in North Africa, and founded part of Phoenicia. Cilix founded Cilicia in Asia Minor, and Thasus established Thassos.

Cadmus traveled across the Mediterranean, making stops at Calliste (Santorini) and Samothrace before reaching the Greek mainland. He journeyed on to Delphi, seeking advice from the Oracle as to how he could recover his sister. The Oracle told Cadmus not to continue the journey for Europa, but instead to establish his own city. This new city's location would be determined if Cadmus followed a cow that had a half-moon on its flank. Where the cow laid down to rest, was where Cadmus needed to build his city.

Confused but obedient, Cadmus left Delphi and soon found the cow with the half-moon. He followed the cow with his small retinue for a very long time. The cow eventually stopped to rest on

the banks of the River Cephisus, in Boeotia.

Cadmus wanted to sacrifice the cow to Athena, so he sent his men out to collect water from a nearby spring. Unfortunately for Cadmus and these men, the spring was a sacred spring which belonged to Ares, and was guarded by a deadly serpent known as the Ismenian Dragon. While his men fought the dragon, it ultimately killed them all.

Cadmus eventually got up to follow the trail when no one returned, and encountered the dragon with the bodies of his men. He attacked the beast in revenge and fought it, eventually killing it. This of course angered Ares, meaning that Cadmus was forced to spend eight years serving Ares as penance.

Cadmus still had to build his city, however the dragon had killed all his men, so he had no one to build it. Athena came to his aid, pleased by the sacrifice of the cow. She told Cadmus to sow half of the serpent's teeth in the ground, and when Cadmus did so, fully grown men emerged out of the ground. Cadmus was afraid of the sudden

ABOVE: *The dragon devouring the companions of Cadmus.* Hendrick Goltzius, 1588. We see the dragon with a soldiers head in its mouth while pinning down another soldier with its claws. In the background Cadmus thrusts a spear down a dragon's throat as revenge for all his soldiers being killed.

OPPOSITE: *Cadmus asks the Delphic oracle where he can find his sister, Europa,* by Hendrik Goltzius. This engraving was published in 1615.

CADMUS Son of King Agenor and Queen Telephassa of Tyre, brother of Cilix, Pheonix, and Europa.

Cadmus is best known for introducing the Greeks to the Phoenician alphabet.

ABOVE: *Cadmus sowing dragon's teeth,* by Peter Paul Rubens, between 1636 and 1700.

presence of so many and threw a rock at them, causing them to fight amongst themselves. In the end, only five survived the skirmish.

These five men became the Spartoi, and they helped Cadmus build his new city, and became the predecessors for all the prominent families in Thebes. Cadmus gave the rest of the dragon's

teeth to Athena, which would eventually become one of the trials of Jason.

Cadmus established his city with the Spartoi, calling the resulting city Cadmeia. To honor the city's creation, Zeus and Athena offered Harmonia to Cadmus for a wife. Harmonia was not a mortal woman, but a minor goddess of

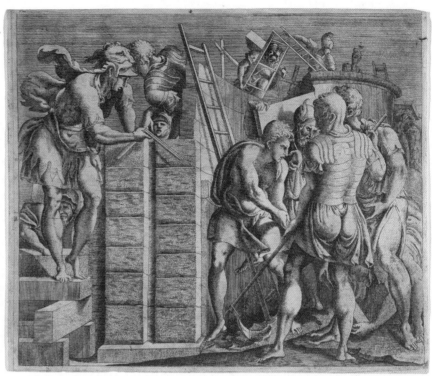

ABOVE: *Cadmus founding Thebes*, by Francesco Primaticcio, between 1543-44.

harmony. Marrying her was a very high honor and their wedding was attended by many gods and goddesses.

Together they had many children, including: Autonoe, the mother of Actaeon; Ino, who became a sea goddess; Semele, the mother of Dionysus; Agave, the mother of Pentheus who became a future king of Thebes; Polydorus, who succeeded Cadmus as king; and Illyruis, who is Illyria's namesake.

Illyria was born outside Cadmeia, as Cadmus and Harmonia would often leave the city to settle various disputes on the border. He became king of the tribes who lived there as well. Illyria became the name of one such border place after his son.

Soon after the birth of Illyrius, Cadmus began struggling with severe depression, and was still plagued by the eight years of service he had promised Ares in penance for killing the dragon. He thought that even a serpent would be happier than he was, so Ares took his final revenge and turned Cadmus into a serpent.

Harmonia was devastated by this, and begged to be given the same fate so that she could remain with her husband. Zeus took pity on them, and moved the transformed lovers to the Elysian Fields, a place in the afterlife that was like paradise, and reserved for those who had found favor with the gods.

A few generations later, during the reign of Amphion and Zethus, Cadmeia would have its name changed to Thebes in honor of Thebe, wife of Zethus. The name Cadmeia would be reserved for the citadel of the city.

CASSANDRA Daughter of King Priam of Troy, and Hecabe (Hecuba). Cassandra had many siblings, the most notable being Hector, Paris, and her twin brother Helenus. Famously given the gift of prophecy.

CASSANDRA

Cassandra was one of the most famous prophetesses in Greek mythology. Apollo had bestowed upon her the gift of foresight, although it would become more of a curse than a blessing.

Cassandra was a mortal princess, and lived in the city of Troy. She was also known as Alexandra, in the same way that Paris is sometimes called Alexander. Cassandra grew up to be the most beautiful of King Priam's daughters, and therefore had many mortal and immortal suitors.

Apollo was one such man, who had an eye on the fair maiden and wanted her for his own. In one version of this myth, Apollo offered Cassandra the gift of prophecy as a courting gesture. Having accepted his gift, she then rejected his sexual advances. Instead of removing this ability, Apollo decided to curse her instead: her prophecies would always be completely accurate and would come to pass, but no one would ever believe her predictions.

Affected so badly by this curse, Cassandra taught Helenus how to see the future, and Helenus managed to become just as accurate and effective with his predictions as she had been, thanks to her capable tutelage.

Another version of the myth is that Cassandra and Helenus were given their prophetic gifts as infants, when they were left overnight in the temple of Apollo. During the night, two serpents found the children and licked their ears, allowing them accurate glimpses of the future. Later, when Cassandra rejected Apollo, he turned her gift of prophecy into the same curse, where no one would believe her despite her accuracy.

Some mortal suitors of Cassandra included Telephus, son of Heracles, whom she would then go on to help wed her sister Laodice. There was also Othryoneus of Cabeus, and Coroebus of Phrygia.

Cassandra really stepped into the spotlight during the events at Troy. She predicted the destruction of Troy when Paris was born, and said he should be killed to avoid the War. Only Aesacus, her half-brother, believed her, and said the same thing. This part of the myth is usually attributed to Aesacus. Cassandra then brought it up again when Paris returned with Helen of Troy, which initiated the Trojan War. She was once again ignored.

Cassandra witnessed many of her brothers die during the war, and when the Greeks concocted their plan of hiding inside the great wooden horse and sneaking inside, Cassandra saw what would happen. She tried to warn everyone of the risk, but of course, she was once again ignored. The wooden horse was taken into Troy, and led to the final massacre.

During the sacking of Troy, Cassandra sought refuge in the Temple of Athena, however she was found in the temple, and raped by Ajax the Lesser. This was one of the acts performed by the Greeks which would result in future problems. They offended many gods and goddesses who had sided with Troy during the war, with the result that they had great difficulty in returning home.

Cassandra became a prize of the war, and became Agamemnon's concubine. She gave birth to Pelops and Teledamus. Despite being Agamemnon's slave, she still tried to warn him of their fate should they return to Mycenae, where Agamemnon was king. Agamemnon's wife, Clytemnestra, was having an affair with Aegisthus, and would murder both of them should Agamemnon return.

Again, Cassandra was ignored, and so they were both murdered when they returned after the War. Agamemnon was murdered by either Clytemnestra or Aegisthus or both, and Cassandra was killed along with her sons by Aegisthus.

There is a less common version of this story, where Cassandra survives. She was not in Agamemnon's company when he returned home, and therefore was not murdered in Mycenae. Instead, Agamemnon gave her, Hecabe, Helenus, and Andromache (her sister-in-law) freedom after the war. They would then go on to make a new home for themselves in Thrace.

ABOVE: *Cassandra*, painted by Evelyn De Morgan, circa 1898.

OPPOSITE: *Ajax and Cassandra*, painted by Solomon Joseph Solomon, 1886.

BELOW: *Cassandra's prophecy of The fall of Troy*, woodcut illustration.

Clytemnestra was the daughter of Tyndareus and Leda, and a princess of Sparta. She was born from one of the eggs laid by Leda after Zeus appeared to her and seduced her as a swan.

CLYTEMNESTRA

Leda produced four offspring from two eggs: Castor and Clytemnestra from one egg, and Helen and Polydeuces (Pollux) from the other. Castor and Clytemnestra were fathered by Tyndareus, whereas Helen and Polydeuces were fathered by Zeus.

Clytemnestra's first husband was Tantalus, King of Pisa. While Agamemnon and his brother Menelaus were in exile and staying at the home of Tyndareus, Agamemnon murdered Tantalus, and Clytemnestra's infant son, and took Clytemnestra as his wife. Menelaus also married Helen around this time.

After Helen was taken to Troy, Menelaus asked Agamemnon for help in the war, but the wind was too weak for the large fleet to set sail. A priest told Agamemnon that he needed to sacrifice his daughter, Iphigenia, to Artemis, and the winds would turn. Agamemnon convinced Clytemnestra to send Iphigenia to him, with the promise that their daughter would be married to Achilles. When Iphigenia arrived, he sacrificed her, and the winds changed and grew stronger, allowing the fleet to set sail for Troy.

The Trojan War lasted for ten years, and while Agamemnon was away, Clytemnestra began an affair with his cousin, Aegisthus.

Whether Clytemnestra entered into this affair willingly, or was seduced, varies according to the author of the myth. They began conspiring to kill Agamemnon. Clytemnestra wanted revenge for her daughter's sacrifice, as well as the murder of her previous family and her subsequent forced marriage. The father of Aegisthus had been betrayed by Agamemnon's father, so Aegisthus had reasons for wanting revenge as well.

There are variations in the myth as to whether Clytemnestra killed Agamemnon herself, assisted Aegisthus, or if Aegisthus was entirely responsible for the murder. However the best known version of the myth is that when Agamemnon returned from the war with his concubine, Cassandra, in tow, Clytemnestra waited until Agamemnon was in the bath, trapped him in a fishing net, and then stabbed him to death when he was unable to untangle himself or resist her attacks.

Cassandra had been cursed that no one would believe her prophecies. She saw a vision of her death, but no one would believe her or assist her, so she walked into the palace after Agamemnon to meet her death as well.

After the murders, Aegisthus replaced Agamemnon as king and ruled for seven years with Clytemnestra as his queen. Orestes, the youngest son of Agamemnon and Clytemnestra, was away when his father returned from Troy.

Legend says that he was rescued by a nurse, and smuggled to safety after Agamemnon's death. When he eventually returned and killed Clytemnestra, he was tormented by the Furies for the crime of matricide, and eventually went mad, fleeing from land to land with no chance of escaping their constant torment.

ABOVE LEFT: The side of a pot showing Orestes holding a knife about to kill his mother, Clytemnestra.

ABOVE: *Clytemnestra*, painted by John Collier, 1882.

OPPOSITE: Clytemnestra hesitates before killing the sleeping Agamemnon.

DAEDALUS AND ICARUS

Daedalus originated from Athens. He was a skilled inventor in the service of King Erectheus, and became famous as a sculptor and Architect. In his workshop, his nephew was his apprentice, a boy called Perdix who invented the saw and the compass.

Daedalus was jealous of the boy's brilliance, and feared his nephew would become more famous than his master, so he flung Perdix off of the Acropolis to his death. Because of this, he was banished from Athens, and went to Crete.

The story of Icarus and Daedalus is a very popular Greek myth. At least, the story of Icarus features heavily in moral storytelling to this day. It is a powerful metaphor for human achievement and hubris. The warning phrase "Don't fly too close to the sun" is an allegory that asks us to reach for the impossible. There is the caveat not to forget caution, and not to become too arrogant.

The story of Icarus begins with him and his father, Daedalus, being locked away in a tall tower next to the sea, but Daedalus had begun his work much earlier. After leaving Athens, he

served King Minos of Crete. At the request of Queen Pasiphae, he constructed a hollow cow so that she, having been cursed to fall in love with a wild bull, would be able to mate with the animal. Thus the Minotaur was conceived and born. Minos then went on to command Daedalus to trap the Minotaur inside a giant labyrinth.

As thanks, Minos threw Daedalus and Icarus into prison. He couldn't kill Daedalus, since Daedalus knew the secret of escaping the labyrinth. Minos kept watch over the sea, so for Daedalus the only escape was the sky. Daedalus was good at making things, and soon constructed a theoretical means of escape.

Daedalus began to gather feathers, and constructed a pair of wings, made of wax and shaped like those of a bird. He fastened them

ABOVE: Marble relief of Daedalus and Icarus.

OPPOSITE: *The Lament for Icarus,* painted by Herbert James Draper, 1898.

ABOVE: Line drawing of Icarus getting too close to the sun and his wings melting and falling off.

OPPOSITE: A painted ceiling in the Louvre museum, Paris, France. *The fall of Icarus*, painted by Merry-Joseph Blondel, 1819. Daedalus looks on in horror as his son Icarus falls from the sky.

together with string and used wax to secure the feathers in place. The wings worked, and so Daedalus gave them to Icarus, as a means of escape. He warned Icarus to be careful – if Icarus flew too low, the waves and sea foam would soak the feathers and make them too heavy. If he flew too high, the wax would melt and the wings would fall apart.

Daedalus had his own pair of wings, and together they set off, successfully escaping the tower. For a while everything was going smoothly, until Icarus forgot himself, lost in the euphoria of flying, and started to climb higher and higher. The heat of the sun melted the wax on his wings, and he fell into the sea, and drowned.

Daedalus realized that Icarus was no longer with him, and he searched the sky and the sea. The body of Icarus washed up on the shore of the island which would then be named Icaria. It had been found and recognized by Heracles, who eventually brought it to Daedalus.

When Daedalus realized that Icarus had fallen, he was consumed with grief. He flew to the kingdom of Cocalus on the southern coast of Sicily. There he hung up his wings and built a temple to Apollo. King Cocalus was impressed by the skill of Daedalus and welcomed him.

King Minos had not forgotten Daedalus, and

had been searching for him since his escape. Word of a great architect living in Cocalus reached him, and Minos, being a clever man, chose not to go to Sicily or even to declare his intention of finding and capturing Daedalus. Instead, he sent King Cocalus a puzzle – was there a way his master craftsman could thread a conch shell?

Daedalus was presented with the puzzle, and came up with a clever way to solve it. He cut a hole in the top of the conch shell and put a drop of honey inside. Then, he tied the string to an ant and set it into the conch shell. The ant twisted all around and through the shell in search of honey, successfully threading it.

That was enough for King Minos to be sure it was Daedalus residing in Sicily, so he set sail for the island. King Cocalus realized the true intentions of Minos, and while he wanted a good relationship with Minos and his people, he prized his fine architect even more. When Minos arrived, rather than hand Daedalus over, he killed Minos instead.

Daedalus continued to live peacefully in Sicily. He went on to build a treasury, an artificial lake, and created a system for warming the water of the public baths, among many other creations.

HECTOR

Hector was the Prince of Troy, and one of Troy's most notable defenders against Achilles, Ajax, Diomedes, and Odysseus during the Trojan War.

During this period Priam was king, having been so named by Heracles years earlier following the death of Priam's father.

Troy prospered under Priam, who had a large number of children with his various wives. His most famous wife was Hecabe, who was the mother of Hector.

There is little told of Hector's life prior to his role in the Trojan War, but his reputation was so great that the opposing heroes knew they would have to defeat him, as he was the mightiest of all the Trojan warriors.

Hector's wife, Andromache, was famously and universally portrayed as the perfect wife, who loved and supported her husband. She pled with Hector not to leave Troy and enter the battles raging outside, but Hector ignored her despite knowing that defeat was inevitable. He put his duty to Troy above his duty to his family. This sense of duty put him in high esteem when his story was later told.

Hector was the one who chastened Paris for eloping with Helen and causing the war, bringing such a large army to their doorstep. When Paris refused to fight Menelaus in single combat, which could potentially have avoided an all-out war, Hector belittled him and called him a coward.

When war was inevitable, he took up arms in defense of his home. Hector was credited with killing the first Achaean hero Protesilaus, who was the first to set foot on the beaches outside of Troy. Despite Hector's best efforts, and that

of Cycnus, the Achaeans managed to secure the beach, unload their ships, and begin the ten-year war.

Throughout the war, Hector was at the forefront of the battles. It was said that he alone killed 30,000 of the Achaean soldiers. Another account says that he alone killed 30 Achaean heroes, including Menesthes, Eioneus, and Trechus.

Hector is, however, most known for his battles against the heroes Ajax the Greater, Patroclus, and Achilles.

After realizing Paris would not fight Menelaus and avoid a war, Hector sought to bring an end to the war himself, and challenged the Achaean army to send their bravest hero to meet him in combat. His reputation was fierce, and it took a long time for someone to step forward, but eventually Ajax rose to the challenge. The fight was long and exhausting, lasting until dusk, with both men proving to be evenly matched. Eventually, Hector and Ajax agreed to call it a draw, impressed by each other's skill and courage, and exchanged gifts. Hector gave Ajax a sword, and received a girdle – both of these gifts would eventually be linked to the demise of their new owners.

HECTOR The story of Hector primarily comes from Homer's Iliad.
Played a starring role in the Trojan War.
Heir apparent and son to Priam, king of Troy, and his wife Hecabe.
Hector's wife was Andromache, a Cilician princess, who bore him a son, Astyanax.

LEFT: A wood carving of Ajax and Hector exchanging gifts.

BELOW: Hector admonishes Paris for his softness and exhorts him to go to war. A painting by Johann Heinrich Wilhelm Tischbein, 1786.

OPPOSITE: *Hector taking leave of Andromache: the Fright of Astyanax.* A pen and ink drawing, by Benjamin West, 1766.

The Trojan War dragged on, with Troy's walls holding out against any attempted breach. However, their allies fell. There was a disagreement between Agamemnon and Achilles when they split their spoils, after which, Achilles withdrew from the battlefield.

The absence of Achilles made the Trojans confident enough to launch counterattacks. One attack almost resulted in the burning of the Achaean ships. Throughout this, Achilles still refused to fight. He only agreed to give his divinely crafted armor to Patroclus, who ensured that the ships were not destroyed.

Achilles expected Patroclus to return after defending the ships, but Patroclus pushed on and eventually battled with Hector. Patroclus did not have the same skill, and Hector killed him by skewering him with a spear. He removed the armor of Patroclus and left his body untouched.

This was enough for Achilles to rejoin the fight, incensed by the death of his beloved friend. He donned new armor and began fighting again. Hector had heard a prophecy that said Achilles would kill him, so to begin with, he stayed behind the Trojan walls. However, his sense of duty soon overwhelmed him, watching so many of his fellow soldiers die, so he once again entered the battlefield to face his fate.

Athena was playing her part in this as well, aiding Achilles and giving him weapons. She also tricked Hector into believing that he had help, only to flee when Hector encountered Achilles. Hector knew that he was to die, so he decided to make it memorable and glorious. He charged at Achilles with his sword, and was struck down by the spear of Achilles when it pierced his neck.

With Hector fallen, Troy's greatest warrior fell, and the city soon after.

Achilles was not assuaged by Hector's death. Grieving for Patroclus still, he wanted to destroy the body rather than return it to Troy. He strung Hector up by his heels, using the girdle of Ajax, and attached it to his chariot. He rode around the city for twelve days, dragging the body of Hector behind him. Despite this, Hector's body came to no harm, because Apollo and Aphrodite were protecting it.

Achilles was given a warning by the gods to end his attempted destruction of the body and instead ransom it. Priam left Troy to seek Hector's body, and managed to get into the tent unseen with the aid of Hermes. Priam begged Achilles for his son's body, and Achilles was moved by his pleas, as well as by the warning from the gods. He allowed Priam to collect the body and return it to Troy for the final time.

Troy mourned Hector's loss, and the two sides agreed on a 12-day truce to hold funeral games in his honor, as had been done for many Achaean heroes.

OPPOSITE TOP: Achilles about to kill Hector, Pallas Athena between them.

OPPOSITE BELOW: *Andromache Mourning Over Body of Hector*, painting by Jacques-Louis David, 1783.

BELOW: A detail from a Roman sarcophagus made of marble, circa 180-200 AD. It shows a scene from the Iliad of Hector's corpse brought back to Troy.

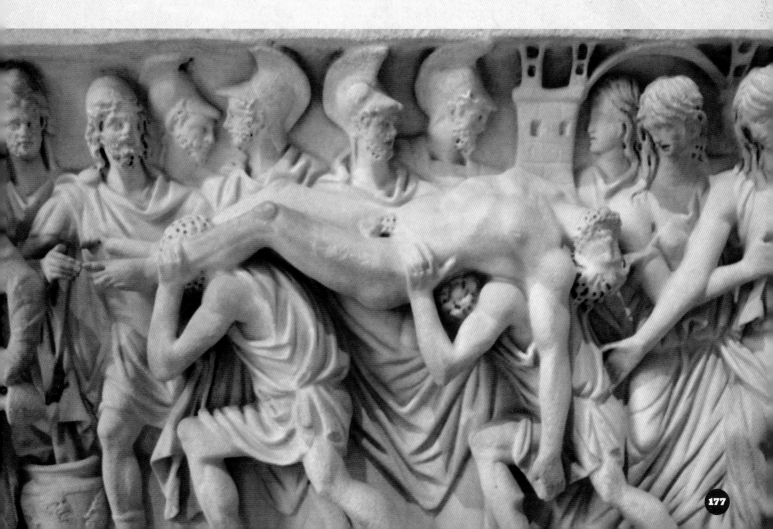

Helen of Troy was considered the most beautiful woman on Earth. Hers was the face that launched a thousand ships.

HELEN OF TROY

ABOVE: Marble bust of Helen of Troy.

ABOVE RIGHT: *Recovery of Helen* by Menelaus, circa 550 BC.

OPPOSITE: A detail from *The love of Helen and Paris*, painted by Jacques-Louis David, 1788.

Despite her name, she was actually from Sparta not Troy, but spent time there and it was her abduction by Paris to Troy which initiated the Trojan War.

There are several versions of her birth origin story. The most famous one is that Leda, the wife of King Tyndareus of Sparta, was seduced by Zeus in the form of a swan. She laid two eggs, one of which hatched to produce Helen and her twin brother Pollux. The second egg produced Castor and Clytemnestra, who were actually the children of Tyndareus.

A second birth story is that Helen was the daughter of Nemesis, who was trying to escape from Zeus and would transform herself into different shapes in order to escape the lustful god. Nemesis turned herself into a goose, and Zeus turned into a swan, making Nemesis lay an egg and abandon it in a forest. A shepherd then found it and took it to Leda, who kept it safe until it opened. She was so taken with Helen's beauty that Leda decided to raise Helen as her own.

When Helen was ten, Theseus and Piritous saw her and fell in love with her. They cast lots to see who would have her, and Theseus won. He kidnapped her and took her to Aphidnae, where he entrusted Helen to Aethra, his mother. Helen's brothers, the Dioscuri, went to retrieve her while Theseus and Piritous were away trying to capture Persephone. They discovered Helen's location and took her and Aethra back. Aethra became Helen's slave until the end of the Trojan War.

In some versions of this story, Theseus impregnated Helen and she gave birth to Iphigenia, who was then brought up by Clytemnestra so that Helen's reputation would remain intact. Other versions say Theseus 'respected' her and she was therefore still a virgin.

When Helen returned home, Tyndareus wanted her to be married. Her beauty had already become renowned and she had suitors from all over Greece. Tyndareus was afraid of insulting all the others by picking one, until

ABOVE: Menelaus is about to strike Helen, but he mesmerised by her beauty and drops his sword. On the left is Aphrodite with Eros flying above.

OPPOSITE: *Helen of Troy*, painted by Evelyn De Morgan, 1898. Helen gazes at her reflection in the mirror which is decorated with a naked Aphrodite.

ABOVE: A fresco found in Pompeii, circa 79 AD. It shows Helen of Sparta being helped to board a ship for Troy.

Ulysses suggested that the suitors swear an oath to respect the choice, and to aid the husband if something were to happen. Helen chose Menelaus, the future king of Sparta, and the other suitors respected the oath they had taken.

At a wedding of the gods, everyone was invited except for Eris, the goddess of discord. She was angry at being left out, so took a golden apple and inscribed it with a message 'for the most beautiful', throwing it into the middle of Athena, Hera, and Aphrodite. Of course, the three proud goddesses immediately began to argue over who the apple's rightful owner was. They asked Zeus to decide, but he didn't want to get involved, so it fell to Paris, a mortal, to decide who the most beautiful of the goddesses was and who should have the apple.

They tried to bribe Paris as well: Hera offered him power and to make him a king; Athena promised wisdom and to be undefeated in battle; Aphrodite said that she would give him a wife, and make the most beautiful woman in the world fall in love with him. Paris, true to classic Ancient Greek male tradition, chose love and said Aphrodite was the most beautiful and should get the apple.

Paris then went to Sparta and stayed as a guest at the court of King Menelaus. Helen saw him and fell in love with him just as Aphrodite had promised. Depending on the version, it's not clear if Helen was abducted or went willingly, but either way, she and Paris promptly left Sparta and set sail for Troy together.

This, of course, prompted Menelaus to call on the oath sworn by the other suitors, who promptly allied with him and went to war with Troy in order to get Helen back, thus beginning the ten-year long Trojan War.

It's a matter of debate as to Helen's behavior during the war. The Iliad states that she would stand on the walls of the city, identifying the Greek kings and telling the Trojans their names. When the Trojan Horse was left behind,

Helen suspected something so she approached the horse and mimicked the wives of the warriors inside. It was with tremendous effort that they remained silent.

In other times, Helen assisted the Greeks. She didn't expose Ulysses when he entered Troy in disguise even though she recognized him, and she later helped him steal the Palladium statue. When Troy fell, she lit a torch to show the Greeks which room she was in so they could find her and ferry her away safely.

After Paris was killed in the war, Helen was given to Deiphobus as his wife, and when Troy was being sacked she hid all his weapons so he couldn't defend himself. Menelaus killed Deiphobus and wanted Helen dead too, but she stayed his hand by exposing her naked shoulder, which made him forgive her immediately.

During their long journey home, they encountered Orestes in Argos, who blamed Helen for all the wrong that had been done to his family. He tried to kill her, but Zeus sent Apollo to rescue Helen and make her immortal, according to Euripides. According to other traditions, Helen and Menelaus returned to Sparta, where she became a model wife.

When the Greeks saw Helen arriving home, they wanted to stone her, but her beauty saved her life again. They were unable to raise a hand against her because of her great beauty.

When Menelaus died, Helen was exiled from Sparta by his sons as a punishment for all the trouble she'd caused. In Rhodes she had a friend, Polyxo, who lived there. However, Polyxo's husband had died in the War, so she had her servants dress up as Furies to frighten Helen as punishment. Helen was so terrified of the ruse that she hung herself.

Yet another legend says that now-immortal Helen and newly immortal Achilles became married and lived happily ever after on the White Island.

HERACLES

Heracles is considered to be the greatest of all Ancient Greek heroes. He was undoubtedly the most famous with his legends being told to this day.

HERACLES IS THE ORIGINAL ANCIENT GREEK NAME OF THE MORE WELL-KNOWN ROMAN VERSION, HERCULES.

Heracles was the son of Zeus and a mortal woman named Alcmene. Alcmene was the granddaughter of Perseus.

Zeus disguised himself as Alcmene's husband, Amphitryon, and slept with her on the same night as her husband. Nine months later, Alcmene bore twins. Heracles was Zeus' son, and Iphicles was the son of Amphitryon. Hera, as she often did, took Zeus' infidelity with intense rage and hatred towards the children, but she didn't know which twin was the son of Zeus.

She sent two snakes into the twins' cradle in secret. Iphicles began to cry at the sight of the snakes, but Heracles strangled the snakes without any fear. Which proved without doubt which of the babies was the mortal one.

Sending the snakes to kill the children was not Hera's intention. She merely needed to know which was the son of Zeus. Before the birth of Heracles, Hera had persuaded Zeus to promise that the next child born to the house of Perseus would become a High King, and that the child who came after would be the King's servant. This wasn't a difficult promise for Zeus to make, because Heracles was supposed to be the next child of Perseus' line.

However, once Zeus promised Hera what she wished, Hera ordered Eileithyia, the goddess of childbirth, to delay the birth of Heracles until the premature birth of Eurystheus. Her plan succeeded, meaning that Eurystheus was destined to be a High King, and Heracles his servant.

Heracles was taught by many, all things that would help him be a great hero. Amphitryon taught him to drive a chariot, and Autolycus, Odysseus' grandfather, taught him to wrestle. The king of Oechalia, Eurytus, taught Heracles archery, and Castor trained Heracles in fencing. Harpalycus of Phanotè, a fearsome son of Hermes, taught Heracles to box.

Linus, who was the son of one of the Muses, taught Heracles how to write and the secrets of literature. He may have also taught Heracles the lyre. Others say that Eumolpus, Philammon's son, was Heracles' music teacher. Heracles certainly had the best of the best to teach him

everything he could possibly need, as the son of a king and demigod destined for great things.

It didn't take long for Heracles to start living up to his divine lineage. When he was 18 years old, he killed the Lion of Cithaeron, a fierce giant lion that feasted on the flocks of Amphitryon and Thespius. Heracles hunted the Lion of Cithaeron for fifty days, and finally managed to kill it. He took its skin and wore it, using the lion's scalp as a helmet, which would then go on to feature in almost all of his artistic renderings and in later legends where he appeared.

Thespiae was so amazed by Heracles' bravery, power, and determination, that he wanted all of his daughters to have a child by Heracles. Thespiae had fifty daughters, and so one by one he sent each of his daughters to Heracles over fifty nights. Because of the similarity of the daughters, Heracles thought he was lying with the same woman each night, and slept with all of them. In that way he sired at least one child with each of the daughters.

On the way back from his successful lion hunt and celebration, Heracles encountered the heralds of Erginus. They had been sent by the Minyan king to collect a tribute of 100 cows, which the Thebans were forced to give every year. Heracles was so enraged by this ridiculous tribute that he attacked the heralds, cutting off their ears, noses, and hands, and fastened the severed limbs to them by their necks, before telling them to carry that back to Erginus and the Minyans.

ABOVE LEFT: Marble head of Heracles.

ABOVE: Heracles as a baby strangling a snake. It had been sent to his cradle by Hera, Zeus' wife, while she was in a rage.

OPPOSITE: The remains of the Temple of Heracles in Agrigento, Italy.

BELOW: A tribute of 100 cows which the Thebans were forced to give away.

Erginus, as one might expect, was angry enough to declare war, and sent the Minyan army to march against Thebes. Unfortunately for them, Heracles was still in evidence and killed Erginus and most of the army, before demanding that the Minyans pay double the original tribute to Thebes.

Creon was the king of Thebes at the time, and was so grateful to Heracles that he gave his daughter Megara, to be wife of Heracles. Heracles was happily married and had many children with her. Hera, was in a jealous rage when she saw that Heracles was making a heroic name for himself. She struck him with temporary madness, causing him to kill his wife and children while he was out of his mind.

To purify himself of this horrible sin, the oracle at Delphi told him to serve Eurystheus, the king of Tiryns, for the next twelve years, and to complete every task that Eurystheus would impose on him. These became the famous Twelve Labors of Heracles.

LEFT: Engraving of Heracles slaying the Hydra.

OPPOSITE TOP: Heracles capturing the Ceryneian Hind.

OPPOSITE MIDDLE: Over the shoulder of Heracles is draped the captured Erymanthian boar, which was his fourth labor.

OPPOSITE BELOW: Heracles fifth labor was to clean the stables of the immortal cattle. Here he lifts a huge rock with his immense strength, in order to divert two rivers to clean the stables.

Joannes Müller

First, Heracles was told to slay the Nemean Lion, which was a monster living in the region of Nemea. It would capture women as hostages and lure brave men to save them. When the men entered the cave to save the woman, the woman would turn into the lion and eat them. The problem was that the lion's skin was impenetrable, so while Heracles shot it with many arrows, none of them pierced the beast's hide. So he followed it into its den and blocked one of the entrances, entering through the other. Heracles stunned the lion with his club and then strangled it to death.

He replaced his first lion skin with the impenetrable one, to use as armor. With the help of Athena, Heracles managed to skin the lion and returned to the Eurystheus victorious.

For the second labor, Heracles had to slay the Lernaean Hydra, which was a fierce monster that Hera had specifically raised to kill Heracles. The Hydra had nine heads, one of which was immortal, and the swamp was covered in a poisonous mist. When Heracles arrived, he covered his mouth and nose with a cloth, and shot flaming arrows to lure the hydra out of its lair. He began to chop off the hydra's heads, but whenever he struck a mortal one, two new heads sprung up in its place.

Iolaus, Heracles' nephew, had come with him on this labor, and so Heracles shouted for his help. Iolaus came up with an idea – whenever Heracles cut off a head, Iolaus would rush forward with hot iron and cauterize the wound, which meant no more heads could grow.

Hera was watching this, and became angry that Heracles was apparently winning. She sent a huge crab to try and distract Heracles, but Heracles simply squashed it with his foot. Heracles made his way to the immortal hydra head, and with a golden sword that Athena had given him, together he and Iolaus cut off and cauterized the wound, killing the monster once and for all. Heracles dipped his arrows in the poisonous blood of the hydra before he left.

Eurystheus, however, said that this labor didn't count as a success, because Heracles had help. So he still had work to do. Eurystheus and

Hera conspired and decided that Heracles' next task would be to capture the Ceryneian Hind, which was a sacred deer belonging to Artemis. It had golden antlers, and hooves of bronze, and was believed to be fast enough to outrun a flying arrow.

Chasing the Hind took Heracles a full year, as it was so fast. He finally managed to capture it while it was sleeping. On his way back, Artemis and Apollo appeared to Heracles. Heracles realised that this task would anger her – and Eurystheus had depended on it – but when they appeared, Heracles explained that this was part of his penance for killing his wife and children. He also told Artemis that he would release the Hind as soon as it was presented to Eurystheus. Artemis accepted his apology, and let him go.

When Heracles presented the Hind, Eurystheus claimed it for himself, but Heracles remembered his promise, and tricked Eurystheus by saying he should bring the animal to the palace himself. When Eurystheus came for the deer, Heracles simply let it go and the animal ran back to Artemis.

Heracles was then asked to capture the Erymanthian Boar. Heracles found himself in the presence of the centaurs, including the wise and immortal Chiron. Chiron told Heracles that he would be able to catch the boar in deep snow, so Heracles chased the beast and caught it during a heavy blizzard. He brought it back to Eurystheus, who was so terrified of the giant animal that he hid in a large jar until Heracles got rid of it.

The fifth labor was to clean the stables of the immortal cattle belonging to King Augeas of Elis, which had not been cleaned in thirty years. Heracles was to clean them within a day. Heracles diverted two rivers through the stables, washing them out. When Eurystheus heard this, he said that the rivers had done the work for Heracles, and refused to acknowledge this labor as a completed one.

The sixth labor was slaying the Stymphalian Birds – huge flying monsters with bronze beaks, metallic feathers, and poisonous dung.

ABOVE: With his bare hands, Heracles captures the Cretan Bull, his seventh labor.

BELOW: The flesh-eating mares that Heracles had to capture for his eighth labor.

They belonged to Ares and had destroyed all the surrounding towns. Heracles was unable to venture into the swamp, as it was too deep. Athena gave him a rattle, which scared the birds and made them fly from their hiding place: he was then able to shoot them down with his poisonous arrows.

Next, Heracles was to capture the Cretan Bull for his seventh labor. He received permission from King Minos to capture the bull, which he did with his bare hands, and sent it back to Eurystheus, who once again hid in his large jar. He wanted to sacrifice the bull to Hera, but Hera rejected it, as she believed this would glorify Heracles' success even more. Instead, Heracles left it in Marathon, where it would later be given the name the Marathonian Bull, and appear in other myths.

For the eighth labor, Heracles was to steal the mad, flesh-eating mares owned by Diomedes, king of Thrace. Heracles managed to capture the mares and on their way back, Diomedes gave chase. While Heracles went to fight the king, his friend Abderus was tasked to watch the mares, only to be devoured by them.

Heracles was so angry that he fed Diomedes to his own horses, after which their madness was cured. Heracles bound their mouths shut and brought them to Eurystheus, who either sacrificed them to Hera, or let them roam free since they were no longer dangerous.

Lots of the labors of Heracles involved venturing into hostile lands to steal things. The ninth labor was no exception. The Amazonian Queen Hippolyta had been given a girdle by her father Ares, and Eurystheus' daughter Admete wanted it for herself. So, he sent the hero on his way to steal it.

When he arrived, Hippolyta had already heard of Heracles' grand deeds, and agreed to come aboard the ship and hear his plea. Heracles told her the story of his madness, the murder of his family, and his attempts to pay penance. She was so moved by his story, and so impressed by his reputation, that she agreed to give him the girdle. At the same time, unbeknownst to either of them, a disguised Hera was telling the Amazons that Heracles intended to capture and abduct their Queen. The Amazons were furious and rushed for the

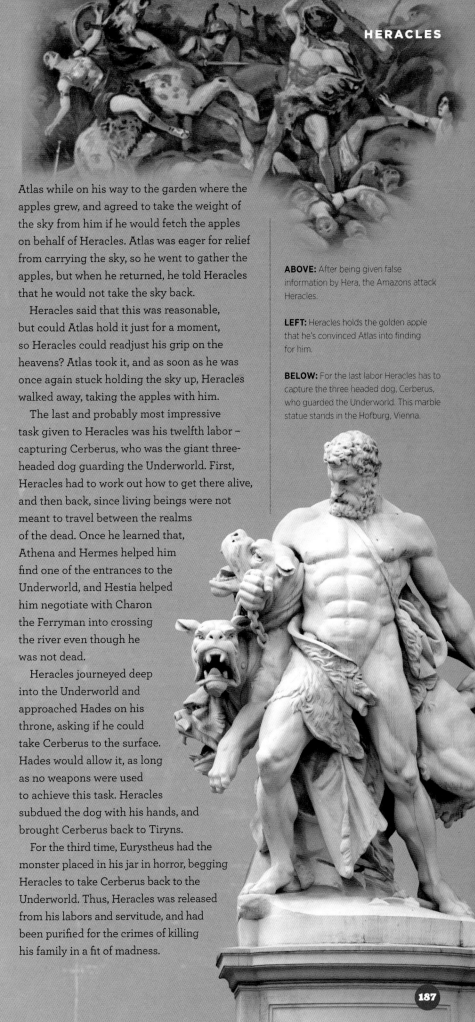

Atlas while on his way to the garden where the apples grew, and agreed to take the weight of the sky from him if he would fetch the apples on behalf of Heracles. Atlas was eager for relief from carrying the sky, so he went to gather the apples, but when he returned, he told Heracles that he would not take the sky back.

Heracles said that this was reasonable, but could Atlas hold it just for a moment, so Heracles could readjust his grip on the heavens? Atlas took it, and as soon as he was once again stuck holding the sky up, Heracles walked away, taking the apples with him.

The last and probably most impressive task given to Heracles was his twelfth labor – capturing Cerberus, who was the giant three-headed dog guarding the Underworld. First, Heracles had to work out how to get there alive, and then back, since living beings were not meant to travel between the realms of the dead. Once he learned that, Athena and Hermes helped him find one of the entrances to the Underworld, and Hestia helped him negotiate with Charon the Ferryman into crossing the river even though he was not dead.

Heracles journeyed deep into the Underworld and approached Hades on his throne, asking if he could take Cerberus to the surface. Hades would allow it, as long as no weapons were used to achieve this task. Heracles subdued the dog with his hands, and brought Cerberus back to Tiryns.

For the third time, Eurystheus had the monster placed in his jar in horror, begging Heracles to take Cerberus back to the Underworld. Thus, Heracles was released from his labors and servitude, and had been purified for the crimes of killing his family in a fit of madness.

ABOVE: After being given false information by Hera, the Amazons attack Heracles.

LEFT: Heracles holds the golden apple that he's convinced Atlas into finding for him.

BELOW: For the last labor Heracles has to capture the three headed dog, Cerberus, who guarded the Underworld. This marble statue stands in the Hofburg, Vienna.

ship. Heracles assumed this had been a trap set up by Hippolyta, so he set her back on shore and took off with the girdle as fast as he could.

For the tenth labor, Heracles was told to steal the cattle of Geryon. The cattle were guarded by the two-headed dog Orthrus, which Heracles killed with his club. He then killed Eurytion, the herdsman, when he tried to confront Heracles. Geryon donned three shields, three helmets, and grabbed three spears, ready to attack the hero. However, one shot from Heracles' bow was enough to pierce his forehead and kill him. Getting the cattle back home wasn't easy, as Hera sent gadflies to irritate and scatter them, and flooded the road home so Heracles had to build a bridge to cross it, but eventually he succeeded in bringing the cattle back to Eurystheus.

Since Eurystheus had claimed two of Heracles' labors were invalid, he was given two more tasks to complete. First, the eleventh labor, which was stealing the golden apples from the Hesperides.

The Hesperides were nymphs, and the daughters of Atlas. Heracles came across

JASON AND THE ARGONAUTS

Jason was the son of Aeson and Alcimede, and he was supposed to succeed his father on the throne of Iolcus after Aeson died. The position was usurped by his half-uncle Pelias around the time Jason was born.

ABOVE: The centaur Chiron teaching Jason how to play the lyre. Roman fresco dated first century AD.

ABOVE RIGHT: Jason's ship *The Argo* painted by Lorenzo Costa, 1500. The Argonauts are setting sail to find the Golden Fleece.

Pelias killed all of Aeson's children, but Jason had been declared a stillborn, and sent to the centaur Chiron which was customary for stillborn children. Chiron, realizing that the boy was alive, raised him to adulthood.

Pelias, in the meantime, learned from an oracle to be wary of a man wearing a single sandal and coming from the country, as that man would be the one who killed him.

Once Jason was an adult, he returned to Iolcus to attend games held by Pelias, in honor of Poseidon. He lost one of his sandals in the river on the way there, while helping a disguised Hera to cross the river.

Hera hated Pelias, since he did not honor her properly, and so she blessed Jason after he had helped her. When Jason appeared in front of Pelias, and introduced himself as the rightful heir, Pelias asked what Jason would do if confronted with a man who would bring about his death.

Jason said that he would send that man to fetch the Golden Fleece, so Pelias did just that. He then promised that, should Jason succeed, the throne of Iolcus would be his.

Jason accepted the mission, and built a boat which would be sailed by a party of heroes. Over eighty men applied for the mission, Heracles among them. They were called the Argonauts, as the ship was named Argo.

At the top of the steps stands Pelias, king of Iolcos. He sees Jason (bottom right) wearing only one sandal. A fresco from the first century AD.

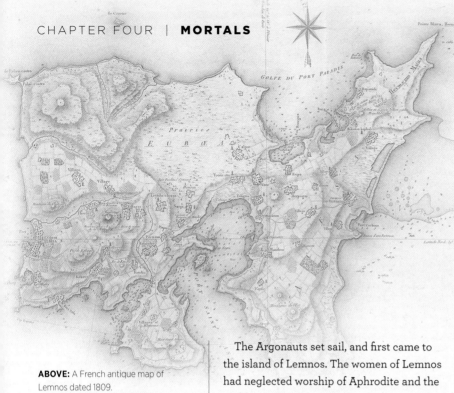

ABOVE: A French antique map of Lemnos dated 1809.

OPPOSITE: An engraving of the Argonauts battling against the storm which eventually pushes them back to the land of the Doliones.

BELOW: *The Harpies Driven from the Table of King Phineus by Zetes and Calais.* Drawing with black chalk, brush and gray wash by François Verdier.

The Argonauts set sail, and first came to the island of Lemnos. The women of Lemnos had neglected worship of Aphrodite and the goddess caused their husbands to spurn them in favor of captured Thracian women. The women in revenge killed all of the men with the exception of Thoas, father of Hypsipyle who was the ruler of Lemnos. The Argonauts remained in Lemnos for a while, sleeping with the women and fathering a new race, the Minyans.

After Lemnos, they sailed to the land of the Doliones, and were warmly greeted by King Cyzicus. While hunting for supplies, their ships were attacked by six-armed giants, most of which were slain by Heracles before the rest of the Argonauts returned and pushed the giants back. They set sail at night, but a wind pushed them back, making the Doliones think they were being attacked by pirates.

The Doliones stormed the ship, and there were many losses on both sides, including King Cyzicus. When dawn broke and they realized they were fighting allies, Jason and the Argonauts were filled with grief and remorse, and held a funeral for Cyzicus.

The next stop for the Argonauts was Salmydessus in Thrace. There, the blind King Phineus was starving to death, as Harpies had moved into the castle, and whenever the king tried to eat, they would swoop down and steal his food. Jason took pity on Phineus and arranged a luxurious feast that would lure the Harpies down. When the Harpies swooped, Calais and Zetes chased them away for good.

Phineas was so grateful for the help that he told the Argonauts the location of Colchis, where the Golden Fleece resided, and told them how to pass through the Symplegades, the Clashing Rocks. These rocks were huge cliffs that would move and crush anything that passed between them. Phineus told Jason to release a dove, to see if it made it through – this would be the omen for the ship's fate. The dove passed without harm, losing only a few tail feathers. This meant that when the Argo passed through, only minor damage was done to the ship.

Eventually, Jason and his Argonauts reached Colchis, and were welcomed by King Aeetes, who possessed the Golden Fleece. Aeetes did not want to relinquish the Fleece, as it was said that if he ever lost possession of it, his kingdom would fall soon after. He pretended to agree, if Jason would do a few small tasks for him first – tasks that were designed to get the young hero killed.

Jason was unhappy with the news, and desperate, but he had the help of Hera. She convinced Aphrodite to bribe Eros to shoot one of his arrows into Medea, who was Aeetes' daughter. Medea in addition to being a princess, was also a high priestess of Hecate well-versed in the arts of magic and sorcery. Eros did as he was asked, and Medea fell madly in love with Jason and resolved to help him with these dangerous, impossible tasks.

First, Jason was to plow a field using the Khalkotauroi, which were two fire-breathing bulls with bronze hooves. Medea gave Jason an ointment to put on his skin that would protect him from the fire, which allowed Jason to get close enough to yoke the bulls and plow the field as asked.

Secondly, Jason was told to sow dragon's teeth in the field. It seemed easy enough, but when he did so, stone men sprang up from the teeth. Medea had told him how to stop the stone men from killing him, and armed with this knowledge, Jason threw a rock into their midst. The warriors didn't know who had thrown it, so they turned on and killed each other instead of Jason. He was the only one left alive.

ABOVE: With two fire-breathing bulls, Jason plows the field. He is protected from the fire by the special ointment Medea has given him to put on his skin.

OPPOSITE: To check they will have a safe passage, the Argonauts send a dove through the Symplegades, the clashing rocks. Once the dove is through safely, they sail the Argo through.

BELOW: Stone men grow from the dragon teeth that Jason has planted. He throws a rock into the middle of them causing confusion. They kill each other and leave Jason unharmed.

Since it was clear Jason would not be killed with these tasks, Aeetes plotted to kill Jason and the Argonauts in the night. Medea sensed this, and fled to the Argonauts, where she then led Jason to a sacred tree where the Golden Fleece was guarded by a dragon that never slept. Medea used her magic on the dragon to make it fall asleep, allowing Jason to take the Golden Fleece and bring it to the Argo.

Medea went on to help Jason kill the giant bronze man Talos, and killed her own brother when he attempted to catch the Argo as it was escaping. Medea killed her brother Apsyrtus and threw his pieces into the sea, causing Aeetes to stop and retrieve them. This caused Zeus to become angry at Medea, and he created many storms to slow the Argonauts' journey back home.

To redeem themselves, Jason and Medea stopped at Aeaea, where the nymph Circe, Medea's aunt, absolved them from the sin. And so, the Argonauts sailed on. They faced many dangers, two of which are particularly notable.

First, they ran into a coven of Sirens, who would sing to sailors and lure their ships onto sharp rocks, where they would crash to their death and be drowned. The Argo, however, had Orpheus on board. When the Sirens began to sing, Orpheus played his music, and his lyre and singing was so beautiful and loud that it drowned out the Siren song, helping the Argonauts to sail past them unharmed.

Talos was a giant man made of bronze who swam around the shores of Crete, defending it from invading ships. Talos would throw stones at anyone approaching. Medea cast a spell on Talos that removed the plug which kept his ichor – the divine blood – in a single vein. This caused him to bleed to death.

ABOVE: A still from the film, *Jason and the Argonauts*, 1963, with Talos, the bronze man, defending the shores of Crete. The terrified Argonauts try to flee the beach.

LEFT: An etching by Jean-Baptiste Nolin of Jason carrying off the golden fleece. On the right Medea holds her spell book in her right hand and uses magic to make the dragon sleep, while Jason steals the golden fleece.

OPPOSITE TOP LEFT: Marble statue of Jason with the golden fleece over his arm. Bertel Thorvaldsen.

OPPOSITE TOP RIGHT: Pelias sits on his throne, in front of him stands Jason holding the golden fleece. A winged victory prepares to crown him with a wreath. This pot dates circa 340-330 BC.

OPPOSITE BELOW: *Circe*, painted by Frederick Stuart Church, 1910. Here she is on the island of Aeaea with her lions, absolving Jason and her neice, Medea, of their sins.

ABOVE: A rejected Medea about to take vengence. She holds her wand in hand ready to wield it against her children, Jason and his new wife. *The Disillusioned Medea* painted by Paulus Bor, circa 1640.

RIGHT: This 16th century drawing shows Medea escaping on a chariot pulled by dragons after she has killed her children, Jason and Glauce, Jason's new wife.

Eventually, Jason and the Argonauts made it home. Many years had passed and Jason found Aeson as an old man. He was distraught, and asked Medea to give his father some of his life. Medea instead slit his throat and let him bleed out, while filling his veins with an ancient elixir. Following this intervention, Aeson woke forty years younger.

Hera, still unavenged, persuaded Pelias' daughters to ask Medea how they could help their own father that way. Medea tricked them into repeating the ritual, but this one had them cutting him into pieces and throwing him into a cauldron – which, of course, proved a little trickier where resurrection was concerned. Pelias met his end, and his son Acastus exiled Jason and Medea from the island.

They ventured on to Corinth, where Jason fell in love with Glauce, King Creon's daughter. Medea confronted him about it, but he ignored her, causing her to fly into a fit of rage. She soaked a robe with poison and sent it to Glauce, who put it on and began to scream from the pain. Her father rushed in to help her, causing him to die from the poison leeching into his system as well. Medea then killed the sons she had with Jason, afraid that Jason would retaliate because she wanted to cause him as much pain as possible.

Medea then fled Corinth, using the chariot of her grandfather, the sun god Helios.

Jason's life did not end happily. In some versions of his myth, he killed himself in despair over what Medea had done. In another version, he eventually recovered the throne of Iolcus, but had lost favor with Hera after breaking his vows to Medea, and without a family, he was a lonely and desolate king.

He died in a very unimpressive way, unbefitting to a hero – while he slept under the stern of the Argo, a rotten beam fell and crushed him to death.

OPPOSITE: Medea has tricked the daughters of their father, Pelias, and they cut him into pieces. *The murder of Pelias by his daughters*, painted by George Moreau de Tours, 1878.

Medea is one of the most famous female characters in Greek mythology. She was a central figure in the quest for the Golden Fleece, as well as being involved in the adventures of Jason and his Argonauts.

MEDEA

ABOVE: Marble statue of Medea carved in 1868.

OPPOSITE: *Jason and Medea* painted by John William Waterhouse, 1907. Here we see Medea making one of her many potions.

Medea was a princess of Colchis, the daughter of King Aeetes and his first wife, the Oceanid Idyia. Medea had two half-siblings, Calciope and Apsyrtus. All three children were grandchildren of the sun god Helios, and Medea was a niece of Perses, and the sorceresses Pasiphae and Circe.

Needless to say, the female bloodline in this particular family was capable of powerful magic. In Colchis, Medea was a priestess to Hecate, the goddess of witches, and was just as skilled at sorcery as her aunts.

The Golden Fleece was in Colchis at the time Jason was tasked to retrieve it, having been brought there by King Aeetes from Phrixus. Aeetes had been told that if he ever lost the Golden Fleece, terrible things would happen to his kingdom, and he would lose it all.

Jason was tasked to retrieve the Golden Fleece and bring it to Pelias, in Iolcus. Jason had the favor of Hera and Athena on this mission, and the goddesses employed Aphrodite's powers to ensure that Medea fell in love with Jason when he arrived. Medea did so, and promised Jason that she would help him retrieve the Fleece from Ares' grove if he agreed to marry her. Jason readily agreed to the arrangement.

ABOVE: Men collect the limbs of Apsyrtus, who has been cut up and thrown overboard. This was Madea's plan in order to slow down Aeetes' fleet of boats and allow the Argo to escape. The frame is surrounded by animals, fruit, scrollwork and the story of Jason and the conquest of the Golden fleece.

There were a number of deadly tasks to be performed by Jason before he could retrieve the Fleece, but for each one, Medea helped Jason succeed. She helped him yoke the fire-breathing bull of Aeetes by giving him a potion that would mean he didn't get burned. She told Jason how to ensure that the Spartoi, the warriors that had been created from dragon's teeth, would kill each other and not him. Medea also put the Colchian dragon to sleep, ensuring that Jason could safely remove the Golden Fleece from the dragon's perch.

Medea was rewarded with by being taken aboard the Argo with Jason and his Argonauts. Aeetes, having discovered that both his Fleece and daughter were gone, sent his fleet in

him. His body was then cut up and thrown overboard into the sea. Aeetes, having caught up at this point, ordered the boats to slow down so they could collect all the body parts of his son, and that allowed the Argo to sail away.

Medea was essential to the Argonauts' safe return to Iolcus. The journey home was long and dangerous, including stops at Circe, where Medea's aunt absolved her of her fratricide. They went onward to Crete, where Medea disabled the giant bronze automaton Talos, that would have otherwise thrown rocks at the ship and destroyed it.

During the return trip, Jason and Medea were married on the island of Phaeacia, which was ruled by King Alcinous at the time. The fleet led by Aeetes had caught up, but as Queen Arete had married the pair, Alcinous refused to surrender them back to Aeetes, and he was forced to give up and return home empty-handed.

They finally managed to return to Iolcus and presented the Golden Fleece to King Pelias. This was a problem for the king, as he'd hoped that the journey would have been disastrous for Jason and his men. What he didn't know was that Jason had Hera's favor, and Hera wanted to punish Pelias. It was her ultimate goal to see Pelias die through Medea's work.

Pelias had promised to relinquish his throne if Jason returned with the Golden Fleece, and when he did not do so immediately, Medea set to work on his daughters. She rejuvenated an old sheep, turning it into a young lamb again by cutting it up, putting it into a cauldron, and then applying herbs to the cauldron. She promised she could make Pelias young again in the same way.

pursuit, and the Argo was unable to outpace the entire fleet.

Medea concocted a plan that would help them keep their lead. She slowed the Argo and allowed a ship that was captained by her brother, Apsyrtus, to pull alongside it. Apsyrtus was allowed to come aboard the vessel, where Medea, or Jason under her orders, murdered

So the daughters of Pelias cut up their own father and placed the pieces in the cauldron. A young and new king did not emerge, the girls had murdered their own father and Medea's magic was not employed to resurrect him.

Pelias' son, Acastus, ascended the throne after Pelias died. Medea could not be blamed for his murder, so Acastus exiled Medea and Jason instead, forbidding them from returning to Iolcus.

Medea and Jason remained in Corinth, and made a new home for themselves. Depending on legend, they had between two and six children together. Where it is said that Medea had two children, then these were sons,

Mermerus and Pheres, but if Medea had six children then there were five sons, Memerus, Pheres, Alcimenes, Thessalus and Tisandrus, and one daughter, Eriopis.

After about ten years, Jason began to resent being married to Medea. In Corinth, those who came from Colchis were said to be barbarians, and this included Medea. Jason arranged instead to marry Glauce, the daughter of King Creon of Corinth.

Whether or not Jason expected to keep this a secret from the sorceress, or assumed she would accept it, Medea reacted as one might expect from a Greek myth: with murder. First, she created a deadly poison and soaked a robe in it, which she then sent to Glauce. The robe was beautiful and Glauce happily put it on, immediately becoming soaked through with the poison. She cried out in pain, causing King Creon to rush to his daughter's aid and remove the robe. However, he died as well because of the poison's secretion entering his blood.

Medea didn't stop there. She then went on to kill Memerus and Pheres, and killed every child except Thessalus. In some versions of the story, their children were killed by the people of Corinth in revenge for the deaths of their king and princess.

Regardless, Medea fled Corinth without Jason, summoning a chariot that was pulled by two dragons which allowed her to escape.

Medea then went on to Athens, which was ruled by King Aegeus at the time. Aegeus desperately wanted a male heir and had tried for years, so that he could pass on the Athenian throne to his son. Medea seduced and wedded King Aegeus after promising that their union would produce a son.

Medea kept her word, and bore Medus into the world. Some claim that this was also Jason's son, but the stories are unclear. Unfortunately for Medea, Aegeus had already fathered an heir – Theseus – he just hadn't been aware of it.

When Theseus arrived in Athens, Aegeus did not immediately recognize him as his own son. Medea did, though, and realized that her son would not become king if Theseus lived. She convinced Aegeus to send Theseus on a quest

to capture the Marathonian Bull, which had previously been captured by Heracles, when it was known as the Cretan Bull. It had since gone mad and was causing death and destruction all around Athens.

Theseus agreed to the quest and successfully captured the bull, bringing it back to Athens as a sacrifice to be made to the gods. Medea tried to kill him again by convincing Aegeus that he was a threat to the throne, and putting poison in his drink. However, before Theseus drank, Aegeus finally recognized Theseus' sword, and that this stranger was his son, and quickly

threw the cup to the floor, saving Theseus' life.

Medea was once again forced to leave her home, taking flight with Medus away from Athens. Since there was nowhere else for her to go, she returned to Colchis, which had changed greatly since she left.

Aeetes had lost the throne due to the theft of the Golden Fleece, and Perse, his brother, had usurped him. Medea intervened so that Perse died, allowing Aeetes her father, once again to become king. Presumably she lived in Colchis happily, and after Aeetes' death, Medea's son Medus became king of Colchis.

ABOVE: Jealous of her husbands second marriage, Medea has killed Glauce, his new wife, and her children. She flees with their corpses on a chariot pulled by serpents. Painted by Germán Hernández Amores, circa 1887.

OPPOSITE TOP: The marriage of Jason and Glauce, daughter of King Creon of Corinth. Pen and Ink drawing.

OPPOSITE BELOW: The side of a pot showing Medea on her chariot pulled by two dragons.

MIDAS

King Midas is most famously the man who wished for the power that everything he touch turn into gold.

ABOVE: King Midas holding his daughter in his arms after turning her into gold. Illustration by Walter Crane, 1892.

OPPOSITE: King Midas, Andrea Vassaro 1670.

This is, a cautionary tale about the dangers of greed and tells of the avaricious King Midas whose wish was granted: he turned his daughter to gold when she embraced him and it led to his demise, because the food he wanted to eat became gold.

That story is adapted from the one the Ancient Greeks told. However, in the original tale, Midas didn't have a daughter, nor did his golden touch cause him to starve to death.

There are three King Midases in history – one in Asia Minor, one in Thrace, and one in Macedonia. To reconcile these three characters, it was said that King Midas lived around Mount Pieria, and that Midas was a follower of Orpheus. His people were known as the Brigians.

The King and his people then moved on to Thrace, then to Asia Minor, where the Brigians became the Phrygians, and allowed for all three of the King Midases to be one person in future stories.

Midas is, of course, the foundation for the term 'Midas Touch', which is usually used in a positive light these days.

The story of King Midas began with the Phrygians, who were without a king. An oracle said that the people should make whoever came through their city gates with a cart into their next king. Gordias was a poor farmer who next came through the gate, some claim he was the last in the royal family line of the Brigians.

Some stories say that he traveled alone, while others say he had his wife with him, and his son Midas. Gordias became king as the oracle advised. He also became the namesake of the Gordian Knot when he tied his cart to the temple with a knot that could not be undone.

In some versions of the tale, Midas' mother was actually a woman who was the daughter of the goddess Cybele, and another man could have been his father. In those versions, Gordias adopted Midas with his wife, or variously, there were two separate kings called Midas whose mythologies were combined.

There is one story of Midas as a child that is not often told. It says that when he was a child in his cradle, ants carried grains of wheat into his mouth. This suggested that Midas was destined to become the wealthiest of kings.

power. His food and drink would turn to gold when he touched them so he couldn't eat. He chased after Dionysus and asked the god to take back his gift.

Dionysus was still feeling a certain benevolence thanks to the safe return of Seilenos, so he agreed and told Midas how to get rid of his golden touch. Midas had to bathe in the head waters of the River Pactolus near the foot of Mount Tmolus. Midas did so, successfully shedding his power and causing a rumor to spread that the River Pactolus carried an abundance of gold.

Therefore, in this version, Midas did not starve or die of dehydration due to his golden touch.

The second most famous tale of King Midas features a musical contest between Apollo and Pan. Pan was a satyr, usually depicted with his iconic pan flute. Pan insisted that his instrument, a syrinx, was superior to Apollo's lyre, so the Ourea Tmolus (the mountain god) was asked to decide between the instruments.

The Ourea Tmolus said that Apollo had won: a decision everyone agreed with except for Midas, who loudly proclaimed that Pan's instrument was the better one. Apollo took offense to this, and wouldn't let the insult go unanswered, so he turned Midas' ears into those of a donkey. After all, only an 'ass' could fail to recognize the superiority of Apollo's music.

Midas returned home and tried to hide his ears between a Phyrgian cap, but of course he couldn't keep it a secret from everyone. The barber who cut Midas' hair had to be made aware, but he was sworn to secrecy.

The barber wanted to tell the secret very badly, but didn't want to break his oath, so he dug a hole in the ground and told the hole Midas' secret. The barber then filled the hole back up. Unfortunately, reeds grew from the hole, and every time the wind blew, the reeds

TOP LEFT: Illustration by Arthur Rackam showing King Midas touching the flowers, they all turn to gold.

TOP RIGHT: Marble statue of Silenus holding grapes in one hand and wine in the other.

ABOVE: King Midas bathes in the River Pactolus in order to break the spell. Illustration by Walter Crane, 1892.

Once an adult, Midas inherited the throne from his father and became king. At this time, Dionysus was traveling from Thrace to Phyrgia. One of Dionysus' entourage was a satyr named Seilenos. He slipped into the garden of King Midas and drank himself into unconsciousness. He was later found by servants, who took the satyr to Midas. Midas welcomed the satyr, giving him food and drink in excess in return for entertainment.

Seilenos stayed with Midas for ten days before being guided back to Dionysus' party. Dionysus was grateful that his friend and tutor was safe and had been looked after, so he granted Midas a wish. Midas, being ultimately human and prone to greedy thoughts, wished that everything he touched would turn into gold.

Dionysus agreed, and gave Midas his fabled golden touch.

Initially, Midas was overjoyed, and turned worthless stones into valuable gold. The novelty soon wore off, however, when Midas discovered the problems with his newfound whispered the secret of Midas and his donkey ears, which meant everyone in earshot heard the king's secret.

When Midas' kingdom was invaded by the Cimmerians, he committed suicide by drinking ox blood. So, his golden touch didn't kill him, or transform his daughter. The Ancient Greeks did not believe Midas had a daughter, but instead had two sons.

Ankhyros would go down in history for his self-sacrifice. When a giant sinkhole opened in Celaenae, Midas asked an oracle what he could do, as many people and their homes had fallen into it and he didn't want the sinkhole to get bigger. Midas was told the hole would close if he threw his most precious possession into it. Midas tried to throw many precious metals and treasures into the hole, but it did nothing. Ankhyros saw his father's attempts, and realized that there was nothing more precious than human life, and so he rode his horse into the hole, which closed around him.

Lityerses is written by historians as the bastard son of King Midas. He was a ruffian who would challenge passers-by to contests and kill those who couldn't win. Eventually Lityerses challenged Heracles, who of course bested him, and beheaded him with his own scythe.

ABOVE: Armorial plate showing the story of King Midas, circa 1520-25.

LEFT: After the musical contest between Apollo and Pan, King Midas said he thought Pan's pipes were superior to Apollo's lyre. Apollo being deeply insulted by this turned King Midas' ears into those of a donkey.

102.   *Midæ ob iudicij craſsitiem aures aſininæ.*

MINOS

King Minos was adopted by Asterion, the king of Crete, along with his siblings Sarpedon and Rhadamanthus. Minos consulted with Zeus, his true father, every nine years, and received his laws directly from Zeus.

His laws were so well-received and successful that after his death he became one of the three judges who presided over the souls in the Underworld and decided their fate according to their race.

When Minos became king, he prayed to Poseidon for a sign that his rule was just and correct. Poseidon sent a pure white bull from the sea, which Minos promised to sacrifice. However, he substituted another bull and did not sacrifice the one Poseidon had sent him. Outraged, Poseidon cursed Minos' wife Pasiphae to fall madly in love with the bull. She commissioned Daedalus to build her a wooden cow, which she hid inside of, and when the bull mated, Pasiphae fell pregnant and gave birth to Asterius, the minotaur. In response, Minos sealed the minotaur in a labyrinth, and imprisoned Daedalus with his son, Icarus, in a tall tower by the sea.

Minos' son, Androgeos, was sent by the king of Athens, Aegeus, to Marathon to fight a bull after his success in the Panathenaic games. Androgeos died during the encounter with the bull, prompting Minos to seek revenge. He went to Athens to avenge his son, and on the way he camped at Megara, where King Nisus, the brother of Aegeus, lived.

Nisus was invulnerable in battle because of a single lock of purple hair he attached to his forehead. Megara was holding strong against the Cretan army until his daughter, Scylla, saw Minos on the battlefield and fell in love with him. Scylla wanted to show her love for Minos, so she removed the lock of purple hair from her father's forehead, causing him to die in battle and ensuring the Cretan victory.

In some legends, it is said that Scylla was bribed by Minos with a golden necklace, and that it was not an act of love. Either way, Scylla performed her task and went to Minos to earn his favor. Minos did not love her, and was repulsed by her betrayal of her father, so he rejected her and sailed away from Megara.

Scylla tried to swim after the Cretan fleet, but soon drowned since she could not keep up with the boats. She was transformed into a small fish, and at the same time Nisus was transformed into an osprey. Nisus flew after his treacherous daughter in a chase that lasts to this day.

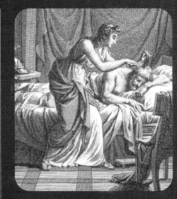

ABOVE: Scylla cuts off her father's purple hair. Drawing by Nicolas-André Monsiau (1754-1837).

After his victory at Megara, Minos sailed to Athens to finish his quest for vengeance. The Athenians were losing the war and submitted to his demands, ordained by Zeus: every nine years, seven boys and seven girls from Athens would be sent to Crete as sacrifices to the minotaur. This would continue until the minotaur's death by Theseus, aided by Minos' daughter Ariadne.

After Daedalus escaped imprisonment, Minos searched for him, traveling from city to city asking a riddle, where he had a spiral seashell and challenged people to string it all the way through. King Cocalus of Sicily, being presented this riddle, fetched Daedalus who was hiding in his court, to solve the riddle. When Daedalus solved it by tying the string to an ant and having the ant walk through the seashell, Minos demanded Daedalus be handed over to him for punishment. Cocalus persuaded Minos to take a bath first, where his daughters, along with Daedalus, trapped Minos in the bath and killed him by scalding him to death with boiling water.

ABOVE: Theseus and the Minotaur. Oil on panel painted between 1500 and 1525.

ABOVE: Minos sits at the entrance of the underworld to decide the fate of all the souls that enter. Each time Minos' tail wraps round a sinner represents one circle further down the sinner must go. Illustration by Gustave Doré, 1857.

ODYSSEUS

Odysseus, the legendary Greek hero and king of Ithaca, was the main protagonist in the Odyssey. The great-grandson of Hermes, he was known for his power of speech, his cunning, trickery, and cleverness.

He went on many adventures and was central to the outcome of the Trojan War. He was also one of the only Greek heroes to be given a long life after his adventures.

His parents were Laertes of Ithaca, a former Argonaut, and Anticlea. When he was a youth, he joined his uncles on a boar-hunting trip, where he managed to kill the boar despite his relative inexperience. He didn't do this cleanly, however – the boar hurt him, leaving a deep and recognizable scar on his leg.

He was one of the suitors of Helen of Sparta, later Helen of Troy and the catalyst for the Trojan War. He was also one of the suitors without much of his heart in it, as he preferred Helen's cousin Penelope, and was certain that Helen's father, Tyndareus, would not choose him as her husband.

Helen had so many suitors that Tyndareus feared insulting them all, so Odysseus came up with a solution: if Tyndareus promised him Penelope's hand, Odysseus advised him to make all suitors swear an oath that they would respect Tyndareus' choice of Helen's suitor, and if Helen's marriage was ever challenged, the suitors would lend their aid to her husband.

The idea worked, and after Menelaus was chosen, all the other suitors peacefully left Sparta – except for Odysseus, who stayed there until Tyndareus kept up his part of the bargain, and convinced his brother to allow Penelope to marry Odysseus.

Odysseus and Penelope returned to Ithaca, and were happily married. They soon had a son, Telemachus. Unfortunately soon after Telemachus was born, Paris abducted Helen of Sparta and Odysseus was called to action by the oath he had sworn, along with the rest of Helen's suitors.

Odysseus didn't want to join the expedition, as the seer Halitherses had informed him that should he join, it would take him a long time to return home. He decided to try getting out of it by pretending to be insane, harnessing both a donkey and an ox to a plow and salting a field. Palamedes, who had been sent to retrieve Odysseus, didn't fall for the ruse. In order to test it, he put Telemachus in front of the plow. Odysseus immediately changed course, saving his son and exposing his madness as fake. Odysseus swore revenge against Palamedes for forcing him to join the expedition and not falling for his ploy. Odysseus' involvement in the rescue mission was crucial and would eventually decide the outcome of the Trojan War.

OPPOSITE: *Odysseus and Penelope*, painted by Francesco Primaticcio, circa 1563.

BELOW: *Odysseus ploughing the sea shore*, an engraving made in 1888. Odysseus attemps to show he's gone mad by using a donkey and ox to plow the shore. Palamedes tests him by putting Odysseus' son Telemachus, on a blanket in the path of the donkey and ox. Odysseus stops to save his son, and proves to Palamedes that he hasn't gone mad.

TOP: *The Discovery of Achilles among the Daughters of Lycomedes*, painted by Jan de Bray, 1664.

ABOVE: Odysseus, on the right, and Diomedes steal the horses of King Rhesus of Thrace who they have just murdered. circa 360 BC.

His involvement began with recruiting the incredible warrior Achilles. Achilles' mother Thetis had heard a prophecy which said that Achilles would die in glorious battle. She feared him dying young, so she had disguised him as a girl and hidden him away in the court of King Lycomedes, who ruled with the island of Scyros.

Odysseus learned that Achilles was in Scyros, and journeyed there to expose his disguise. Achilles presence was essential, as Odysseus had been told by a prophet that it was the only way they could win the war. He disguised himself as a peddler selling women's clothes, but also laid a spear among his goods. Achilles,

who was going by the name of Pyrrha, was the only one who showed interest in the spear. Another version of the story is that Odysseus feigned an attack on Scyros, and exposed Achilles as he was the only person who did not flee after hearing the battle horn.

Odysseus' main role was as a strategist and advisor. He was singularly good at maintaining morale and managed to prevent the Greeks withdrawing after Agamemnon tried to test them by allowing them to leave. Odysseus was also a capable warrior. Together with Diomedes, he captured the Trojan spy Dolon and killed him, as well as King Rhesus of Thrace. He also captured Helenus, the Trojan seer, to learn what needed to happen for Troy to fall. The conditions necessary included the recruitment of Achilles' son Neoptolemus, as well as Philoctetes who possessed Heracles' bow and arrows. Odysseus went on to play a central role in bringing both of these men in to fight for the Greeks.

Of course, Odysseus' main and most memorable contribution was the invention of the Trojan Horse. The War had been going on for ten years, and was at an impasse. Odysseus had a giant hollow horse constructed and hid the army inside, leaving it near the Gates of Troy and feigning a withdrawal with the Greek fleet. The Trojans believed the horse was a divine animal, and saw it as a sign from the gods that the war was over and that they had won.

They wheeled the horse into the Gates, and when night fell, the Greek army slipped out of the hollow animal and launched a brutal attack on Troy. They opened the Gates for the rest of the army to come through, and burned Troy to the ground, thus finally ending the War.

Odysseus never forgot his grudge against Palamedes. He faked a letter that falsely exposed Palamedes as a traitor, which led to Odysseus and Diomedes stoning him to death.

ABOVE: A marble bust of Neoptolemus, son of Achilles.

BELOW: The Procession of the Trojan Horse in Troy, painting by Giovanni Domenico Tiepolo, circa 1760.

TOP: Odysseus and his men in a battle with the Cicones. Study for a fresco, Francesco Primaticcio, 1555-60.

ABOVE: Odysseus rescuing his men from the lotus-eaters, after they had eaten the fruit and forgotten everything. Theodoor van Thulden, 1633.

After the war, it took another ten years for Odysseus to reach home. Along the way he had many additional adventures. He left Troy with twelve ships, and a strong wind drove them off course. They found themselves among the Cicones south of Thrace, who were allies of Troy. There was a battle, where Odysseus and his men killed all the Cicones except for a priest of Apollo, named Maron.

Maron was grateful that his life was spared, and gave Odysseus twelve jars of strong wine. Odysseus and his men stayed a little too long in celebration, drunk on the wine, which gave the Cicones enough time to summon reinforcements. They overpowered Odysseus' crew, killing six men from each of the twelve ships.

Odysseus escaped with the rest of his men and landed in the realm of the Lotus-Eaters. Three men went to scout ahead, but none of them returned – this was because the Lotuses that grew on the island had a powerful magic, enough to make men forget their tasks, their homes, and themselves. Odysseus had to drag his scouts back to the ships by force, and then sail on.

ABOVE: Odysseus drives a burning stake into the eye of Polyphemus. Engraving by Bartolomeo Crivellari, 1756.

Next, Odysseus encountered Polyphemus, who was one of the Cyclopes, and a one-eyed giant who tended sheep. Polyphemus had many resources to plunder, but when Odysseus and his men ventured in, Polyphemus blocked off the exit to the cave and started eating his men two by two.

The monster devoured six men before Odysseus concocted a plan of escape. He introduced himself to Polyphemus, calling himself 'Nobody', and then gave Polyphemus some of the wine Maron had given him. He got the giant so drunk that he managed to blind him by piercing his eye. Polyphemus cried out in pain, but when his fellow Cyclopes listened in, all he could yell was 'Nobody is hurting me! Nobody tricked me!' So they couldn't be blamed for not rushing to his aid.

Odysseus then hid with his men under the bellies of the sheep, so that Polyphemus was unable to tell what they were, and let them out to pasture by mistake. Odysseus and his men raced for their boats, but not before Odysseus let slip his true identity to Polyphemus. This was a mistake, as Polyphemus' father was Poseidon, the god of the sea. Poseidon was so angry for what had happened to his son, he sent storms and winds to rage against Odysseus' ship. This in turn delayed his return to Ithaca by another ten years.

Aeolus, the god of the winds, was their next stop. He welcomed them and harbored them for a month. He then put all the wind except for the West Wind in a leather bag, which he gave to Odysseus, to help him on his journey home. Everything was going well until Odysseus fell asleep the day before they were due to reach Ithaca. His men, thinking the bag contained gold, opened it and released the winds. The ships were violently blown back to Aeolus, who realized Odysseus had to be cursed and refused to help him a second time.

Seven days later, Odysseus reached the island of the Laestrygonians, a tribe of bloodthirsty, man-eating giants. The Laestrygonians sank eleven of Odysseus' ships with massive boulders and spears and devoured the sailors on those ships. Eventually, Odysseus made his escape with the crew on his ship, and they were the only survivors.

Odysseus reached Aeaea, which was an island ruled by the sorceress Circe. Circe was surrounded by wild animals, which the story strongly implies were other men she had transformed, as she was quick to turn Odysseus' crew into pigs. Hermes aided Odysseus by giving him a magical herb, which allowed him to resist Circe's witchcraft and attack her. Circe was so impressed by Odysseus' courage that she became enamored of him, and agreed

ABOVE: Circe changing the companions of Odysseus into beasts. Etching by Giovanni Benedetto Castiglione, 1650–1651.

RIGHT: Odysseus receives a leather bag from Aeolus with the winds in it. Etching by Bartolomeo Crivellari, 1756.

to turn his men back. Odysseus and his crew remained on the island for a year, during which time he and Circe became lovers.

Circe told Odysseus to venture into Hades for advice from the seer Teiresias before continuing his journey. There, Odysseus encountered Agamemnon, Achilles, Heracles, and his mother's spirit, who told him to hurry home, as Penelope was being courted by other suitors since Odysseus had been gone for so long. Odysseus rushed back to his ship after Circe warned him that there were still many hardships to come.

His first test was the songs of the Sirens. Circe had warned him that they would sing to him and his crew to entice them onto the sharp rocks, where they would be drowned. Odysseus ordered his crew to stuff their ears with beeswax, and tied himself to the mast, so that he could escape unharmed while still being able to hear the beautiful Siren's song.

Then, Odysseus had to pass through a narrow strait, which was located between the whirlpool Charybdis and the six-headed monster Scylla. He managed, but Scylla ate six of his men for the trouble.

The island of Thrinacia was their next stop. Circe and Teiresias had warned Odysseus of this place, so he cautioned his crew not to eat the cattle there, which belonged to the sun god Helios. However, in his absence, they did, which enraged Helios. He asked Zeus to punish them, or he would take the sun to the Underworld. Zeus obliged, and sent a violent storm that killed everyone but Odysseus.

ABOVE: The companions of Odysseus stealing the oxen sacred to Apollo

BELOW: Odysseus at the table of Circe. James Parker, line engraving, 1805.

BOTTOM: Odysseus is tied to the mast of his ship to prevent him being lured by the sirens. Painting by John William Waterhouse, 1891.

ABOVE: *The return of Odysseus* by E. M. Synge, 1909.

LEFT: *Hermes ordering Calypso to release Odysseus*, painted by Gerald de Lairesse, circa 1670.

Now alone, Odysseus traveled on to Ogygia, an island where the witch Calypso fell in love with him, and kept him prisoner for seven years. Odysseus continued to dream of Ithaca, and would not be swayed, even when Calypso offered him immortality to remain with her. Finally, through the intervention of Zeus and Hermes, at the end of the seven years, Odysseus was released.

He then arrived at Scheria, where the Phaeacians lived. There, Odysseus recounted his adventures during a feast, and the Phaeacians were so happy to have someone of his greatness with them, that they gave him a ship and a new crew, who finally managed to get the exhausted hero back to his home, Ithaca.

Odysseus was asleep when they arrived, so the Phaeacians carried him to the shore and left him there. When Odysseus awoke, he was confused, but Athena appeared to him and told him what had happened. She disguised him as an old beggar for his safety, and so that before revealing himself, he could learn of the changes which had happened in Ithaca during his absence.

Odysseus became the character of the old beggar man, and went to the hut of his most faithful servant, Eumaeus. Eumaeus welcomed him warmly, but did not recognize him. During this time, Odysseus' son Telemachus was sailing home from Sparta. He was ambushed by Penelope's suitors, and having escaped, headed straight for Eumaeus' hut. Odysseus revealed himself to Telemachus and father and son were joyfully reunited.

Odysseus then went with Telemachus and Eumaeus to his house, where the ringleader of Penelope's suitors, Antinous, mocked him and tried to goad him into a fight with Irus, who was another beggar at the palace. Penelope appeared, prompted by Athena, and announced that she was ready to remarry. Odysseus was glad to hear this, as it led him to believe that Penelope had been faithful all these years, and so he made himself a friend of Penelope, still disguised as a beggar.

Odysseus and Telemachus massacre Penelope's suiters, painted by Thomas Degeorge, 1812.

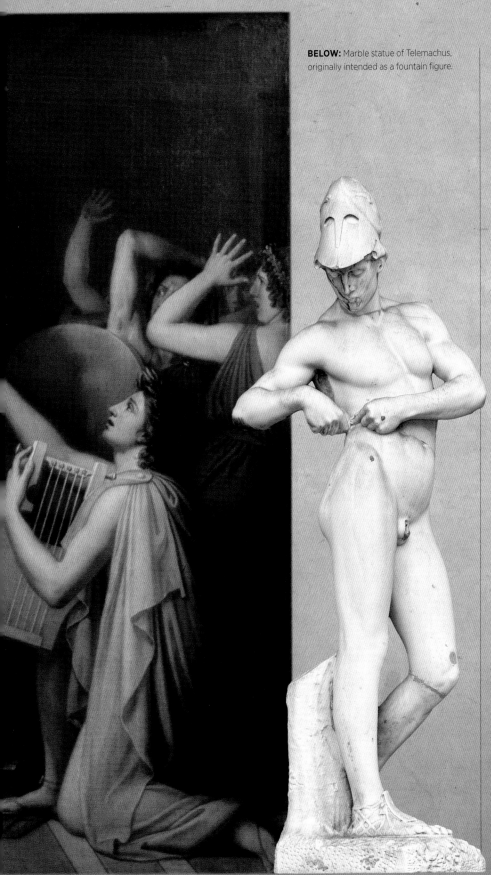

BELOW: Marble statue of Telemachus, originally intended as a fountain figure.

Penelope was so fond of Odysseus that she called Eurycleia – Odysseus' one-time wet-nurse – and asked her to wash the beggar's feet. However, during this task, Eurycleia recognized the scar on Odysseus' leg that the boar had given him as a youth, and realized who he was. She tried to tell Penelope, but Odysseus and Athena worked to keep the secret safe.

Penelope, with the advice of Odysseus, said that she would marry the man who could string her husband's bow, and then shoot that bow with an arrow that would penetrate through twelve ax shafts. No one managed until Odysseus, still disguised, completed the task and revealed himself.

With the assistance of Athena and Telemachus, Odysseus killed all the suitors, and hung the household staff which Eurycleia identified as traitors. Penelope could not believe that this beggar was her husband, even after he had shed his disguise and wore his normal royal garb again.

She was cautious, so asked Odysseus to move their marriage bed to another room. He replied saying that he could not do it, because one of the legs was a living olive tree, and it was deeply rooted in the ground. That was enough proof for Penelope, who ran into Odysseus' arms, and they both wept for joy.

There are a lot of contradictory stories regarding Odysseus' death. Some say that he and Penelope lived happily ever after, while some believe that Penelope *had* been unfaithful, and Odysseus killed her when he found out, before going to another kingdom and marrying Callidice there.

The most famous story concerns his son, Telegonus who was born of his relationship with Circe. Once Telegonus was an adult, he went to Ithaca to meet Odysseus. When he landed, he killed some sheep because he was hungry. Odysseus came out to confront him, and was wounded in the fight with the tip of a poisoned spear.

After finding out that he had killed his own father, Telegonus took both Penelope and Telemachus to Aeaea, where Circe made all three of them immortal.

OEDIPUS

Oedipus is one of the most famous and well-known figures in Greek mythology; the King of Thebes, the Slayer of the Sphinx, and of course, the origin of Freud's famous 'Oedipus Complex', which is still used as a common psychological term and trope in fiction to this day.

ABOVE: The oracle who Oedipus went to visit to find the truth regarding his parents. *Priestess of Delphi*, by John Collier, 1891.

Oedipus is one of the classic Greek tales of a tragic 'hero' doomed from the start. Many prophecies were told of Oedipus, beginning in Thebes, where the current king Laius ruled with his wife Jocasta. Though Laius and Jocasta were desperate for a child, an oracle told Laius that his son would be his murderer. Laius resolved to abstain from lying with Jocasta, but after one drunken night with his loving wife, Oedipus was conceived.

Laius decided to kill Oedipus before the baby could grow up and murder him. A common method of ridding oneself of unwanted children was to expose them on a mountain. Mount Cithaeron was chosen to be Oedipus' resting place. Laius went so far as to pierce his son's hands and feet with spikes to speed up the process.

However, a herdsman was on the mountain, and heard the baby's cries. The herdsman was a citizen of Corinth, which was ruled by King Polybus and his wife, Periboea. The herdsman brought Oedipus to Polybus and Periboea, who took him in and gave him the name 'Oedipus', which translates to 'swollen feet'.

They raised Oedipus as their son, as they had no children of their own, but as Oedipus grew up it became obvious that Polybus wasn't his biological father. His adopted parents refused to tell him the truth, so Oedipus sought answers from the Oracle of Delphi.

Oracles were not well-known for their transparency when answering questions. The Oracle told Oedipus that if he returned to the land of his birth, he would kill his father and sleep with his mother. That it was his destiny. Oedipus, having no reason to think otherwise, believed that the Oracle was referring to Polybus and Periboea, and because he didn't want to harm his beloved 'parents', he resolved not to return to Corinth.

Oedipus left Delphi and began to travel towards Thebes, where he encountered King Laius, his real father. Both of them were strangers to each other, and happened to be on a stretch of road too narrow for both parties to pass at the same time.

Polyphontes, who was driving Laius' chariot, ordered Oedipus to move to one side, and when Oedipus didn't obey quickly enough, he became

ABOVE: The killing of king Laius by Oedipus on the road from Corinth to Thebes, by Joseph Blanc, 1867.

BELOW: *Oedipus and the Sphinx*, by Jean Auguste Dominique Ingres, 1808.

angry and killed one of Oedipus' chariot horses as punishment. This prompted Oedipus to kill Polyphontes and Laius in retribution.

Oedipus had killed his father, as the prophecy foretold.

As he was unaware that he had killed the King of Thebes, Oedipus traveled on, annoyed but unbothered by the encounter. By the time he reached Thebes, the city was being ravaged by a Sphinx, and had no king to turn to in their hour of need.

A Sphinx was a powerful creature, unable to be harmed by a mortal weapon. The only way to banish one was to outsmart it in a game of riddles. If one gave an incorrect answer, the Sphinx would kill the challenger. Many had tried and so far no one had been able to best her.

The current regent of Thebes was Jocasta's brother, Creon. He promised that whoever managed to rid Thebes of the Sphinx would become king and marry Jocasta. Once Oedipus heard this decree, he took it upon himself to face the Sphinx.

The Sphinx was a creature with a lion's body, a woman's head, and powerful wings of an eagle. It had made a nest for itself outside of the city, where Oedipus ventured to face it.

There are two versions of the Sphinx's riddle:

"What goes on four feet in the morning, two feet at noon, and three feet in the evening?" or "Which creature has one voice and yet becomes four-footed and two-footed and three-footed?"

For either version, the answer is 'Man', because a baby crawls on all fours at the 'morning' of a man's life, walks on two legs as an adult, and then has a cane in the 'evening' of old age. Oedipus answered the riddle correctly, prompting the Sphinx to abandon Thebes and render the city once again safe.

True to the decree, Oedipus was pronounced King of Thebes and went on to marry Jocasta, his biological mother, thus fulfilling the second part of the Oracle's prophecy.

Oedipus and Jocasta would go on to have four children – two sons, Polynices and Eteocles, and two daughters, Ismene and Antigone.

Despite having saved Thebes from the blight of the Sphinx, his rule was plagued by disease, famine, and all kinds of misfortune. This was because of Oedipus' patricide and further sins against nature by sleeping with his mother: punishments sent by the gods for crimes of which Oedipus was unaware. Though Oedipus sought answers from the Oracles as to why his rule was so cursed, it wasn't until King Polybus died that Oedipus learned the truth.

Periboea revealed that Oedipus was adopted, and that he was found on a mountain, maimed, and left for dead. Periboea's story, as well as additional evidence, was enough for Oedipus to realize that his true biological parents had been Laius and Jocasta.

Oedipus, upon learning this truth, rushed home only to find that Jocasta had already committed suicide. She knew that Oedipus would find out the truth and it was said she hung herself out of shame. Oedipus then blinded himself with Jocasta's brooches.

Now unfit to rule Thebes, he was succeeded by his sons, Polynices and Eteocles. However, they were so ashamed of their father that Oedipus was kept in the castle and unable to escape, so that no one else could learn the truth. Oedipus cursed his sons for this, and prophesized that violence would plague the brothers.

Eventually, Oedipus was sentenced to exile. Polynices and Eteocles decided that they would alternate their rule over Thebes to avoid violence over their right to rule. Oedipus' daughter Antigone, accompanied him out of Thebes to Colonus, which was under the rule of the King of Athens. Theseus, who was king at the time, welcomed Oedipus and allowed him to stay there.

War did erupt between Polynices and Eteocles, and it was foretold that the son who won the war would have Oedipus as an ally. Oedipus however cursed both of them and refused to align himself with either son, still proclaiming that they were destined to kill each other.

His prophecy did come true; Polynices and Eteocles ended up killing each other fighting for the throne. Oedipus remained in Colonus and was buried there. Although most claimed that he died of natural causes, some believe that Oedipus killed himself after learning of his sons' fate.

Despite the fact that these emotions did not motivate Oedipus' actions, the case of him killing his father and marrying his mother has been used in archaic psychology as a name of a 'complex' where a son might share the desire to do the same out of jealousy towards his father and love for his mother.

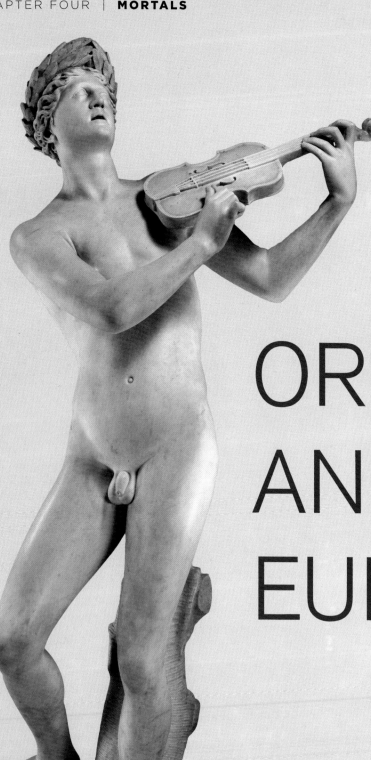

The son of the god Apollo, and the muse Calliope, Orpheus is known as the most talented musician in ancient times.

ORPHEUS AND EURYDICE

Orpheus mastered the lyre as a young boy and had a voice so beautiful that no god or mortal could resist it, and even trees and rocks would move themselves to get closer to his music.

Orpheus is also credited with teaching mankind writing, medicine, and agriculture. He was said to be a seer, astrologer, and founder of many mystic rites. It was said that his music had the ability to expand people's minds and open them up to new theories and information.

Orpheus also played a significant role in the expedition of the Argonauts. He played a lullaby for the 'sleepless dragon', which allowed Jason to steal the Golden Fleece. The music of Orpheus saved the Argonauts from the power

LEFT: Orpheus playing his lyre. Marble statue made between 1600 and 1601, in Florence, Italy.

BELOW: Eurydice steps on a snake which proves fatal. Made of marble, carved circa 1515-1524 by Antonio Lombardo.

of the Sirens, female-like sea creatures that sing songs to lure sailors to their deaths. They would seduce men with their voices to get them to sail their ships into sharp rocks, or jump into the water to be drowned, but Orpheus' music was more beautiful than their song and saved Jason and his men.

Orpheus dedicated much of his life to music and poetry, and soon enough his voice and talent had gained attention of all living and inanimate things, near and far. At one particular concert, a wood nymph called Eurydice, who was beautiful and shy, was drawn to Orpheus' music and instantly fell in love with him. It was love at first sight for Orpheus as well, and the two quickly became completely enamored with each other, refusing to separate.

They were married with the blessing of Hymenaius, the god of marriage. The feast was a grand and joyous affair, the celebration lasting well into the night. However, such happiness wouldn't last. Aristaeus was a shepherd who desired Eurydice for himself and despised Orpheus for stealing her away. The shepherd plotted to conquer her and steal for her himself.

On the way home from their wedding feast, Aristaeus waited in hiding with the intention of ambushing them and killing Orpheus. When he made his move, Orpheus took Eurydice's hand and they both took off running through the forest. The chase lasted for a long while, but eventually Eurydice stumbled and fell. She had stepped on a nest of snakes and been bitten by a deadly viper, which killed her. The shepherd gave up the chase once he realized Eurydice was dead.

After the death of Eurydice, Orpheus was overwhelmed by grief. He no longer sang and found no joy in music or poetry anymore. Eventually, his grief became so powerful that he decided he could go to the Underworld and try to get her back. Orpheus asked Apollo, his father, to treat with Hades, who was god of the Underworld, to listen to Orpheus' plea and accept his request.

Orpheus took his lyre to Hades and requested entry to the Underworld. Hades did not challenge him. Orpheus made his case to Hades and the three judges of the dead. He played a song for Hades and Queen Persephone, begging for Eurydice to be returned to him.

It is said that Hades openly wept at the grief in his voice, Persephone's heart melted, and even Cerberus, the giant three-headed god guarding the entry to the Underworld, covered his ears with his paws and howled in despair. They were so moved that Hades promised Orpheus that Eurydice would follow him back to the world of the living – but there was a catch. Orpheus must not, under any circumstances, look back to Eurydice while she was still in the darkness, otherwise she'd be condemned to stay in the Underworld forever. Orpheus must wait until Eurydice was in the light.

Orpheus began the journey back to the surface, confident that he would be able to complete the task. He could hear Eurydice behind him, running to catch up with him, and while he wanted to look back to her, he controlled himself as best he could. It was very difficult for him to resist the urge, but he made it to the surface and the light.

Unfortunately, he turned around too soon. Eurydice hadn't made it into the light yet, so he only caught a glimpse of her because she was swallowed by the darkness forever. Heartbroken, Orpheus tried to go back and made a second attempt, but the gates to the Underworld were shut and Hermes was standing guard, refusing to let him in.

Orpheus was so full of grief by his loss that he lost all joy and passion for life. He found no happiness in anything, including the companionship of other women. Eventually he shunned humanity entirely, spending hours lying on a huge rock and staring at the open sky.

A group of women, furious that he had shunned them and no longer sang love songs, happened upon him. They killed Orpheus and cut him into pieces, throwing him and his lyre into the river. The Muses eventually found the pieces of his body and his lyre, and gave him a proper burial.

Orpheus' soul went to the Underworld where he could be reunited with his beloved Eurydice. People believed that music could be heard coming from his grave and that it was beautiful and plaintive.

TOP RIGHT: Qrpheus, returning from Hades without Eurydice. Made by Marie Alexandre Lucien Coudray, 1893-1899.

ABOVE: A moment too soon, when Orpheus glances behind him to see Eurydice, and she disappears back into the underworld. Painted by Christian Gottlieb Kratzenstein-Stub, 1806.

OPPOSITE: *Wounded Eurydice*, by Jean-Baptiste Camille Corot, 1868.

PANDORA

Pandora was the first mortal woman, who was crafted out of clay by the order of Zeus, with the intention of bringing misery to mankind.

The Titans Prometheus and Epimetheus had created the first generation of mortal men, as bade by Zeus after his victory against Cronus and his allies. Prometheus loved his creations dearly and wanted to bring them wisdom and comfort, however his actions often angered Zeus. Prometheus tricked Zeus into taking the second-best parts of a sacrificial bull so that mankind could have the best parts, and raided the gods' workshops to steal fire for man, which prompted the ire of Zeus on more than one occasion.

Zeus eventually did exact his revenge on Prometheus, but first he sought to punish mankind, since he knew that would also hurt Prometheus since he loved man so dearly.

With that in mind, Zeus had Hephaestus make a woman from clay, and Zeus breathed life into her. Once she was created and living, Athena gave her clothes, Aphrodite bestowed on her grace and beauty, and Hermes gave her the power of speech. The Charities and Horai gave her additional beautiful accompaniments. Other gods gave her the ability to lie, as well as cunning, and Hera gave her curiosity. They named her Pandora, which means 'all-gifted'.

Zeus sent Pandora to Epimetheus, who was not as forward thinking as his brother Prometheus, and despite warnings from Prometheus not to take gifts from the gods, he

saw and desired her and immediately, made Pandora his wife.

Pandora had brought with her a storage jar, later called a box or chest. She was warned to never open the box, but because Hera had given her such powerful curiosity, Pandora eventually succumbed to it, and opened the box to look inside. Even the slightest opening allowed the dark contents inside it to pour out and flow into the world.

RIGHT: *Prometheus, Mercury, and Pandora*, painted by Josef Abel, 1814. Pandora, on the left, holding pithos, Mercury next to her with his winged helmet. Prometheus is seated holding a torch trying to keep Pandora away from man, the clay figure on the right.

BELOW: *The Creation of Pandora*, by John D. Batten, 1913.

Pandora's Box contained every evil in the world, including suffering, disease, war, and greed. Pandora quickly closed the box but these things had already leaked out in the short time through the small opening. The only thing left inside Pandora's Box was Hope.

Just as Zeus desired, Pandora had damned mankind to a life of struggle when it had previously been easy thanks to the gifts of Prometheus. This introduction of evils would eventually force Zeus to release the Great Flood to wipe out mankind, because wickedness had so distorted mortal men.

In an alternative telling, Pandora was not created as a bid for revenge on Prometheus, but because the gods wanted to prove that they could make a better creation than Prometheus. However the attributes they had given to Pandora, were the things that brought struggle to mankind.

Pandora, with Epimetheus, became mother to the first actual mortal-born woman: Pyrrha. She went on to marry Deucalion, son of Prometheus, and they became the ancestors of the next generation of mankind after the Great Flood.

LEFT: Pithos, found in Crete circa 675 BC. In earlier stories it was called a storage jar (pithos), later referred to as a box or chest.

BELOW LEFT: The moment when Pandora opens the box as curiosity has got the better of her. Engraving by Nicolas Henry Tardieu, 1719.

BELOW RIGHT: *Pandora opening her box*, painted by John William Waterhouse, 1896.

Perseus was the son of Zeus and Danae, making him a half-god, and one of the greatest heroes in Ancient Greek mythology.

PERSEUS

TOP RIGHT: Perseus and his mother Danae being cast out to sea. Engraving by Giorgio Ghisi, 1543.

BELOW: The side of a Greek pot showing Danae and the shower of gold.

He was most famous for slaying Medusa, though in a close second he also killed the sea monster Cetus while rescuing Andromeda.

Andromeda eventually became the wife of Perseus, and bore him one daughter and six sons. One of these sons was Electryon, who fathered Alcmene, who went on to sleep with Zeus and produced Heracles. This made Perseus both Heracles' great-grandfather, and

half-brother, because Greek lineage is nice and straightforward like that.

King Acrisius was told by an oracle that he would be killed by his grandson. In order to defy the oracle, he locked up his daughter Princess Danae, so that she would not be able to marry and have offspring. Zeus appeared to Danae in the form of golden rain which had leaked through a crack in the roof. Danae's father Acrisius found her nursing a baby boy and refused to believe that Zeus had fathered the child. He had them both locked in a box which was thrown in the sea.

Danae and Perseus survived the attempted murder, and the chest eventually arrived at Seiphos, which was ruled by King Polydectes. Dictys, his brother, caught the chest in his fishing net, and freed Danae and her son. Dictys offered them refuge in his house, where Perseus grew up to be a strong young man.

Dictys endeavoured to shelter his new guests from the rest of the island, and succeeded for a long time. It was years before Danae and Perseus were discovered. This was fortunate for as soon as Polydectes saw Danae, he fell in love with her. He attempted to woo her and asked for her hand, but she was timid and repeatedly denied him.

Polydectes took this well but undaunted he redoubled his efforts to woo Danae. Perseus was the only obstacle between him and Danae, so he

ABOVE: *Perseus and the Graeae*, painted by Edward Burne-Jones, 1892. Perseus is leaning over and taking their one eye.

devised a plan to get rid of Perseus.

Polydectes claimed that he was to marry Hippodamia, who was the daughter of the king of Pisa. Her name meant 'tamer of horses', and so each citizen of Seriphos was obliged to bring a horse as a wedding present. Perseus could not afford one, so he went to the king and said he would bring anything else, anything Polydectes desired, as a wedding gift.

Polydectes asked for the head of the Gorgon, Medusa. He was certain this would cause the young man's death, as Medusa's stare had the power to turn anything that looked at her into stone.

Perseus set out on his quest, wandering for days as he looked for the Gorgon lair, but no one knew where it existed. The gods were merciful towards him, and Athena and Hermes appeared to him and told him the Graeae, who were sisters of the Gorgons, would tell him where Medusa could be found.

The Graeae were three old, grey women who shared a single eye and tooth between them. In order to force them to answer him, Perseus grabbed the eye and tooth and promised to give it back if he was given directions. The Graeae had no choice, and told him to go north, where the nymphs knew the location of the Gorgons, and would give him tools to help him slay Medusa.

These northern nymphs were much more hospitable. They gave Perseus winged sandals, a magical bag in which to hold Medusa's head, and Hades' helmet of invisibility.

ABOVE: Perseus killing the sea monster Cetus in order to save Andromeda from being sacrificed. Painted by Edward Burne-Jones, 1888.

RIGHT: Marble statue of Perseus holding up the head of Medusa, which he has just cut off.

OPPOSITE TOP: The story of Perseus killing the sea monster Cetus. On the left Andromeda is tied to a tree ready to be sacrificed. We see Perseus flying above the monster, top right, and then standing on the monster's back about to kill him. By Piero di Cosimo, 1510 - circa 1515.

Armed and ready, Perseus set out. Hermes had also given Perseus an adamantine sickle to cut off Medusa's head, and Athena had given him her bronze shield, which had a powerful ability to reflect, so that Perseus could peer around corners without risking meeting the monster's eyes.

Perseus found Medusa asleep, and struck her, beheading her in one blow. He quickly stuffed her head into the magical bag and made his way back to Seriphos. On his way back, he encountered the Titan Atlas and used Medusa to turn him into a giant stony mountain. Whether this was because Atlas didn't want to grant Perseus hospitality, or because it was an act of mercy to relieve Atlas of his burden, is unclear.

In Africa, Perseus happened upon the good King Cepheus, whose daughter was to be sacrificed to the sea monster Cetus because her mother had boasted that she was more beautiful than all the Nereids.

Perseus fell in love with Andromeda at first sight, and so told Cepheus that if he was allowed to marry her, he would slay the beast and save her. Cepheus agreed, and Perseus flew over the monster's head when it appeared, using his winged sandals, and turned the creature to stone with Medusa's head. Cepheus gladly gave Andromeda in marriage to Perseus. Within a year the couple had their first child, Perses, the ancestor of all future Persian kings.

Upon returning to Seriphos, Perseus learned that Polydectes had continued to harass his mother, and so he used Medusa's head to turn the king and all his attendants to stone. Perseus then returned the divine items he had been given, and gave Medusa's head to Athena, who turned it into the emblem in the center of her shield.

Now, of course, one mustn't forget the original prophecy regarding Perseus and his grandfather. Perseus journeyed with Danae and Andromeda to Argos with the intention of making peace with Acrisius, but when Acrisius heard that Perseus was coming, he fled to the Pelasgian land.

When Perseus couldn't find Acrisium on Argos, he journeyed on to the Pelasgian land where he stopped to compete in the athletic games. He threw a discus and accidentally hit an old man who was standing nearby, killing him on the spot. That old man was Acrisius, thus the prophecy was fulfilled.

Perseus knew what he had done, even though it was an accident. He buried his grandfather outside of Argos, but was too ashamed to go back and ask for the throne. So he went to Megapenthes, who ruled Tyrins, and swapped the thrones. Perseus became king of Tyrins, and Megapenthes, became king of Argos.

Perseus then went on to establish Mycenae, and he lived with Andromeda happily for many years with their children.

ABOVE: Fresco found in Pompeii. Andromeda has a chain around her wrist, attached to a sea cliff. Perseus has just killed the sea monster, and is about to free Andromeda. Notice Medusa's head in Perseus' pocket.

THESEUS

Theseus was conceived on the night his mother, princess Aethra, slept with her husband, Aegeus King of Athens, and Poseidon, god of the sea, so Theseus' father is unknown.

Aethra raised Theseus away from Athens, in Troezen, where he did not know his kingly or possibly divine parentage.

Aegeus was a childless king, even after two wives. He had three brothers, and feared that they would try to usurp or overthrow him since he had no heirs. He went to Pythia, seeking the advice of the oracle to see if he would ever have a son. The oracle gave him an incredibly helpful metaphor that Aegeus didn't understand. Defeated and still not knowing the answer, he headed home, and stopped at Troezen on the way and asked king Pittheus if he would help decipher the oracle's words. Pittheus was famously wise and understood the oracle's words perfectly, but used this knowledge to his advantage – he knew Aegeus would have a male heir, but would not know it until a much later date. He decided to arrange for Aegeus to meet his daughter, Aethra. Aethra slept with Aegeus whom Pittheus had made drunk, a few hours before Poseidon also slept with her. Aethra later gave birth to Theseus.

Whether Theseus was a demigod or merely the son of a very great king, he was truly exceptional as a youth and growing into adulthood. When Heracles once visited Pittheus' kingdom with the lion skin, he took it off before sitting at the dinner table. The children of the palace thought it was a real lion and fled in fear, but Theseus calmly took an ax, approached the skin, and attacked it. Aethra watched this happen and knew her son was destined to be a great hero.

After Aegeus had slept with Aethra, he hid his sword and a pair of sandals beneath a giant rock, and told her that if she bore him a son in nine months, and if he was able to lift the rock, she must send him to Athens with this sword and these sandals, and he would know that the boy was his son and future king of Athens. When the time came, Aethra took Theseus to the rock and told him that story. He lifted the rock with ease, and with his father's sword and sandals, made for Athens finally to meet the mighty king.

Aethra begged Theseus to travel by sea, as the land was full of dangers such as bandits, monsters, and all manner of evil things that would want to do him harm. Theseus refused, as he wanted to earn a reputation of a hero before he met his father, and so purposely chose the more dangerous path in the hopes of proving himself.

OPPOSITE: Theseus finding the sword and sandles of his father. Painted by Laurent de La Hyre, circa 1635-1636.

ABOVE: This Greek bowl, circa 440 BC, shows the encounters Theseus had on his journey to Athens to find his father. In the center Theseus is killing the Minotaur.

By the time he reached Athens, he already had a reputation to rival the fame of Heracles. His first encounter on the way was with Periphetes, the Club Bearer. He resided on the road near Epidaurus, and would savagely beat any traveler who crossed paths with him. When he challenged Theseus, Theseus grabbed Periphetes' club out of his hands and beat him to death with his own weapon. He then took Periphetes' club and continued to use it on his travels.

Next, Theseus encountered Sinis, the Pine Bender, before leaving the Peloponnese. Sinis was infamous for tying travelers to bent over pine trees, and then releasing the trees, which would snap upright so quickly that the unfortunate traveler would be torn in two. Theseus managed to capture Sinis and tied

him to his own trees, ripping Sinis in two and ending his reign of terror.

Typhon and Echidna, largely recognized as the parents of all monsters, had a child named Phaea, the Crommyonian Sow, which was a huge wild pig that wreaked havoc around Corinth and Megara. It's possible she wasn't a literal pig, merely a vicious female robber whose nickname was 'The Sow', but that depends on the story. Either way, Theseus happened upon her and killed her when he realized she was a destructive force plaguing the land.

Barely further on his journey, Theseus encountered Sciron the Foot Washer, who was a mighty brigand. He would force travelers to wash his feet, then kick them off the cliffs into the sea, where they would then be devoured by a giant sea turtle. Theseus was forced to wash his feet, but realized he would soon become turtle food. In the middle of washing, when Sciron lifted his foot, Theseus took hold of the brigand's foot, lifted him up, and hurled him into the sea to be eaten by the turtle.

Cercryon the Wrestler was another one of those people who waited on a road and tried to kill random travelers who came his way. He would challenge people to a 'wrestle or die' contest, which he could win without a problem, except that on this occasion, Theseus was his opponent. Theseus bested him in the wrestling match, and then killed him, thereby completing the challenge.

The sixth and last notable encounter was between Theseus and Procrustes, the Stretcher. Procrustes would pose as a kind, friendly host, who would offer his house as shelter for any traveler that needed it. His house had a short bed and a long bed, which the traveler would have to choose to lay down in. Whichever one they chose, Procrustes made sure they would 'fit' the bed, either by stretching the traveler out, or using hammers to shorten them. The story doesn't detail which way Theseus gave Procrustes a taste of his own medicine, but he either stretched or hammered the seemingly welcoming man to death, ending him once and for all.

Finally, Theseus arrived at Athens. Unfortunately for him, Aegeus had remarried since then, his new wife being the sorceress Medea, who had her own son with Aegeus that she wanted to inherit the throne. She recognized Theseus and knew he was a threat to her son's inheritance.

ABOVE: A sketch for a tile design, *Theseus and the Minotaur in the Labyrinth*, by Edward Burne-Jones, 1861.

BELOW: A bronze statue of Theseus slaying the Minotaur, Antoine-Louis Barye, 1843.

Medea moved quickly, and convinced Aegeus to send Theseus after the Marathonian Bull to prove his worth. This bull was actually the bull that Heracles had to capture for his seventh labor, and was formerly the Cretan Bull. Theseus mastered the volatile bull and sacrificed it to Apollo.

Medea hadn't expected Theseus to be successful, so she sought to poison Theseus. However, just before Theseus was to drink the poisoned cup, Aegeus recognized the sword and sandals he had left behind so long ago, and threw the cup from Theseus' hand, saving his life. He then named Theseus his rightful successor, and banished Medea from Athens.

Settled in and making himself at home, the time came for Aegeus to pay the third yearly tribute to Minos, the king of Crete. This was because it had been established as payment for the death of Androgeus, son of Minos, who had been killed by Athenians out of jealousy. Athens would send fourteen of its noblest young men and women to Crete, where they were to be thrown into the Labyrinth, constructed by Daedalus, to contain the monstrous half-man half-bull Minotaur.

Theseus was still hungry for fame and glory, and hated that so many young Athenians were suffering this way, so he volunteered to go to Crete. Once there, Ariadne, Minos' daughter, fell in love with him. She was determined to assist him and so begged Daedalus to tell her the secret of the Labyrinth, and he eventually agreed. When it was time for Theseus to enter the Labyrinth, Ariadne gave him a ball of thread that Daedalus provided her with, which would help Theseus navigate the Labyrinth to find a way out.

Theseus, armed with the knowledge that he would be able to find his way out, went deeper into the Labyrinth in search of the Minotaur. The Minotaur was huge and monstrous, but it was no match for the strength of Theseus, and so after a brief fight, Theseus killed the Minotaur and made his way safely out of the Labyrinth.

Theseus had promised he would marry Ariadne if he survived. After they married, they left Athens with the rest of the young Athenians who were meant to be sacrificed that year.

Unfortunately, Theseus only remained married to Ariadne for a few days. They were on Dia, when Dionysus arrived a short time later. Dionysus wanted Ariadne for himself, so he carried Ariadne off in his chariot to be his immortal, beloved wife, leaving Theseus behind.

Theseus had promised his father Aegeus that he would change his sail to a white one if he was safe, but it would remain black if he had died. He forgot to change the sail back, so when Aegeus saw a black sail on his son's ship, he became so consumed with grief that he threw himself off of the cliffs, into the sea. Theseus then became the king of Athens. According to most, he was the greatest king, who managed to unify Attica under Athens. He instituted the festival of the Panathenaea and the Isthmian Games, as well as succeeding in many other great accomplishments.

During his reign, Theseus became friends with King Pirithous. They shared many adventures, including the hunt for the Calydonian Boar, and an expedition among the Amazons, which almost eliminated the race of centaurs. During the wedding of Pirithous, the

He pushed Theseus off the highest cliff from which he fell to his death.

The last mention of Theseus came at the time of the Persian War, where Athenian soldiers claimed to see the ghost of the mighty hero, clad in armor and leading the charge during fighting.

The Athenian general Cimon was commanded by the oracle at Delphi to find the bones of Theseus and bring them back to Athens. He did so, and the gigantic skeleton of Theseus was reburied in a magnificent tomb in the heart of Athens, which thereafter served as a sanctuary for the defenseless and the oppressed of the world.

LEFT: A bronze statue of Theseus fighting the centaur Bianor, Antoine-Louis Barye, 1849.

BELOW: *Ariadne abandoned by Theseus*, Thomas Rowlandson, circa 1790.

centaurs became very lively and tried to make off with his fiancé, as well as several female guests. Theseus reached for an ancient bowl near him and managed to smash it in the face of the centaur who had made off with Hippodamia, Pirithous' bride-to-be. The blow cracked open the centaur's skull and mixed with his blood on the sand. He was one of many centaurs to die at the hands of Theseus, without whose substantial help, the King and his allies would have likely fallen to the brutal and capable warriors.

The end of Pirithous came while the two men were inspired to try and kidnap Persephone from the Underworld. Instead of capturing Persephone, they became bound to two enchanted seats with magic chains they could not break.

Fortunately, Heracles was on his way to capture Cerberus, the three-headed dog that guarded the gates of Hades. He discovered Theseus and Pirithous and recognized them. He managed to free Theseus, but when he tried to free Pirithous, the ground shook so badly that they were forced to leave him behind.

Once freed from the Underworld, Theseus returned home to Athens, only to find that Menestheus was now the ruler. Theseus fled to Lycomedes, the king of Scyros, which turned out to be a mistake, because Scyros supported Menestheus. After a few days of fake hospitality, Lycomedes took Theseus on a tour of the island.

TANTALUS

Tantalus, sometimes referred to as 'King of Phrygia', was either married to Dione, one of the daughters of Atlas; Eurythemista, a daughter of the river god Xanthus; Euryanassa, daughter of Pactolus, or Clytia, the child of Amphidamantes and Eupryto.

Tantalus was also the father of Dascylus, and the great-grandfather of Atreus, Agamemnon, and Menelaus.

Tantalus was one of the sons of Zeus, with Pluto the nymph of Mount Sipylus, He was a favored son of Zeus and was given the Sipylus region to rule. With Dione (or any of his other wives depending on the author), Tantalus fathered Niobe, Pelops, and Broteas.

As one of the favorite sons of Zeus, Tantalus was invited to many banquets as a welcomed voice, but he often did not realize how lucky he was to be so well-received. Misdemeanors would begin to build up against him, as Tantalus would often return to the mortal world and spread gossip about what had happened at the banquet tables.

Tantalus would also attempt to steal nectar or ambrosia from the feasts in an attempt to make himself immortal. He was accused of stealing a golden dog which Hephaestus had crafted for Rhea, to guard over Zeus when he was an infant. In some accounts, his friend stole the dog and gave it to Tantalus for safekeeping, where he then lied about having seen or heard of such a thing. In another version, Tantalus stole the dog and hid it with his friend before being questioned and discovered. The worst crime, however, was when Tantalus invited the gods to a banquet which he hosted himself.

For whatever reason, Tantalus decided that he would sacrifice his own son, Pelops, at this feast. He then cut up, cooked, and served his son as a meal to the gods. Most of the gods realized the truth before eating, but Demeter, who was distracted by the fact that Persephone was in the realm of Hades, took a mouthful of the offered food.

Zeus was so angry at the act that he ordered the Furies to resurrect Pelops, which they did by recooking the meal in a magical cauldron. However, part of his shoulder was missing as Demeter had eaten it. To replace the missing body part, Demeter had Hephaestus craft a replacement shoulder from ivory.

As punishment, Tantalus was removed from his throne and Pelops replaced him. Tantalus was then sentenced to eternal torment in Tartarus. Infanticide and cannibalism were considered some of the more heinous crimes in Ancient Greece. Tartarus, which was the Greek version of actual Hell, full of torment and suffering, was deemed the only suitable place for Tantalus to be sent.

Odysseus bore witness to the suffering of Tantalus; he was made to stand in a lake of water that came to his chin, beneath an orchard of trees that bore every kind of fruit. Above Tantalus was a tentatively balanced stone. If Tantalus tried to lower his mouth to drink the water, the water would recede out of reach,

ABOVE: After commiting infanticide and cannibalism, Tantalus was sentenced to Tartarus forever. Hendrik Goltzius, 1588.

OPPOSITE: The feast of Tantalus, where he feeds his son Pelops to the Gods. Hugues Taraval, 1767.

TANTALUS
Name translates to 'he who has to bear much'. Not only a person in history and mythology, but there may have also been an Anatolian city named Tantalis, of which Tantalus was the ruler.

ABOVE: Tantalus eternally condemned to be unable to eat or drink. Engraving by Giulio Sanuto, circa 1557.

OPPOSITE: Atreus after cutting up Thyestes children, feeds them to his guests.

and if he tried to reach upwards for food, wind would blow the branches out of reach. Tantalus was cursed to go forever hungry and thirsty, and the stone would provide anxiety for the rest of time due to a fear that it would eventually tumble onto him and kill him.

The curse of Tantalus didn't end with him, but carried through many generations of his descendants. The House of Tantalus was also known as the House of Atreus, which was a

family line famous for being cursed by the gods. The children of Tantalus were punished for their own individual crimes as well as those of Tantalus himself.

Broteas burst into flame when he offended Athena, Niobe boasted that she was a better mother than the goddess Leto, causing her 14 children to be slaughtered by Apollo and Artemis in retribution. Niobe ended up being turned into a weeping stone because of the loss.

Pelops succeeded Tantalus as king of Sipylus, but was driven out when Ilus invaded. Pelops then traveled to Peloponnesus and married Hippodamia. However, his curse continued when he caused the murder of his potential father-in-law, and killed his own accomplice.

Hippodamia gave birth to Atreus and Thyestes, who would later be exiled for the murder of their half-brother, Chrysippus. Atreus and Thyestes eventually ruled over Mycenae, but a disagreement between the two of them ended with Atreus killing the sons of Thyestes and serving them as food.

Atreus was killed by his nephew, passing the curse to two great-grandsons of Tantalus: Agamemnon and Menelaus. Agamemnon was killed by his own wife, Clytemnestra, who was then killed by their son, Orestes. Orestes was the one to end the curse by praying to Athena and being judged by the court of the Erinyes.

ment edipus mourut.

Auelineline chapitre qui en matie

THE TROJAN WAR

The Trojan War was fought for ten years between the city of Troy and the Greeks, after Paris of Troy abducted Helen from Sparta. In legend, the Trojan War happened as a result of a competition between the goddesses Hera, Athena, and Aphrodite.

RIGHT: A statue of Paris lifting Helen with Menelaus trying to separate them from underneath. Vienna, Austria.

Eris, the goddess of discord, was angry at the goddesses that she had not been invited to a wedding, so she threw a golden apple between the three goddesses, and the apple was labeled to be owned by 'the fairest'.

Paris was chosen to be the judge of the fairest goddess. Hera promised Paris power, Athena promised wisdom, and Aphrodite promised him love. Paris chose Aphrodite, and awarded her the apple, so Aphrodite kept her promise and gave Paris the love of Helen of Sparta, who was considered to be the most beautiful of all mortal women.

Hera and Athena were both angered by the decision of Paris, and so when Paris and Helen ran away together, Menelaus her husband, called upon all the kings and princes of Greece to wage war upon Troy.

One of the most iconic names in the Trojan War is that of the hero Achilles. Achilles was the son of Peleus and Thetis, whose wedding Eris had been barred from attending. It was foretold that one of the children of Thetis would become greater than his father, so while Zeus was in love with Thetis and wanted to have children with her, he promised her to Peleus instead.

For Achilles, it was foretold that he would either die of old age, after an uneventful life, or die young on a battlefield, and gain immortality through poetry. When Achilles was nine, another prophecy was told which said Troy would not fall without the aid of Achilles. There are two common legends regarding Achilles' invulnerability: one was that Thetis would hold Achilles over a fire every night to burn away his mortality, and rub him with ambrosia during the day, until Peleus put a stop to it. Another tale is that Thetis bathed Achilles in the river

Styx, but because she held him by his heel, it was his single remaining point of vulnerability.

Before Menelaus had married Helen, her father had been worried over potentially angering one of the many suitors by rejecting all but one. Odysseus told Helen's father to make every suitor swear an oath that they would defend the marriage no matter who was chosen. They all agreed. Because of this, when Paris stole Helen away, Menelaus was able to call upon the oaths of the other suitors as allies in the war, after diplomacy failed. As a result, he was able to recruit Agamemnon, Ajax, and Odysseus.

In the end, the Achaeans' (Greek) fleet numbered one thousand ships, which is one of Helen's most well-known descriptors: the face that launched one thousand ships.

The war lasted for ten years, during which time many heroes fell, including Achilles and Ajax, as well as Hector and Paris on the Trojan side. Eventually, the War ended due to the ruse of the Trojan Horse.

ABOVE LEFT: *The death of Hector*, Peter Paul Rubens, 1630.

ABOVE: Statue of a man with the dead body of a boy, identified as Achilles and Troilus. 2nd century AD.

BELOW: *The rape of Helen*, Tintoretto, 1580.

Odysseus was the one who concocted the Trojan Horse plot. Horses were sacred to the Trojans, and so he knew that they would not refuse a gift in that animal's shape. The giant wooden animal was built by Epeius, who was guided by Athena, out of trees that grew in a grove sacred to Apollo. The Horse was inscribed with the phrase: "The Greeks dedicate this thank-offering to Athena for their return home", as a further implication that the Greeks had given up the war and left Troy to its own devices.

The horse, however, was filled with Greek soldiers, who waited until the Trojans pulled the horse inside their city. Odysseus led the stealthy forces, while the rest of the army burned their camp and sailed to Tenedos.

The Trojans fell for the ruse, believing that the Greeks had left and decided the War wasn't worth fighting. They dragged the horse inside their city walls so that it would be safe while they decided what to do with the large structure. Some wanted to burn it, some wanted to throw it from a cliff, while others wanted to keep it whole and dedicate it to Athena, as the inscription declared it was meant for.

Cassandra the prophetess warned against keeping the horse. She had been given the gift of foresight by Apollo, but also was cursed by Apollo so that no one would believe her prophecies. The Trojans decided to keep the horse, and they celebrated well into the night. When it was midnight, an Achaean spy named Sinon, signaled that the Trojans were all asleep, and the soldiers inside emerged from the horse and ransacked the city. The massacre was so thorough that it continued well into the next day.

The Trojans fought back desperately and fiercely, but they were disorganized, caught by surprise, and without leaders after the long war and their night of revelry. Some of them stole Greek soldiers' uniforms after the enemy had fallen and launched counter attacks in their disguises, while others hurled roof tiles and anything else heavy they could spare onto the attackers in the streets. In the end, they were overrun, and the Greeks killed or enslaved every citizen before destroying the rest of the city.

ABOVE: View of burning Troy, Johann Georg Trautmann.

OPPOSITE: The Trojan horse, by Motte, 1875.

The Titan's Goblet, Thomas Cole, 1833. Notice how the rim of the goblet has dense vegetation with the remains of classical ruins on either side. On the surface of the water boats sail, and waterfalls cascade from the edge. The scale of the goblet puts into proportion the size of us mere mortals.

INDEX

CREDITS